SUMMER CAMP

GREAT CAMPS OF ALGONQUIN PARK

SUMMER CAMP

GREAT CAMPS OF ALGONQUIN PARK

Text: Liz Lundell

Photography: Beverley Bailey

Concept & Design : John Taylor & Robbie Sprules

A   B O S T O N   M I L L S   P R E S S   B O O K

DEDICATION
For every parent who ever sent a child to camp—especially mine.

Lundell, Liz, 1959-
SUMMER CAMP: GREAT CAMPS OF ALGONQUIN PARK

ISBN 1-55046-092-7

1. Camps - Ontario - Algonquin Provincial Park - History.
2. Camps - Ontario - Algonquin Provincial Park - Pictorial works.
3. Outdoor recreation for children - Ontario - Algonquin Provincial Park - History.
4. Outdoor recreation for children - Ontario - Algonquin Provincial Park - Pictorial works.
5. Algonquin Provincial Park (Ont.) - History.
6. Algonquin Provincial Park (Ont.) - Pictorial works.

I. Bailey, Beverley, II. Title.
GV195.C3L8 1994 796.54'2'09713147   C94-930285-6

Copyright 1994
Photographs: Beverley Bailey
Text: Liz Lundell
Concept and Design: Taylor/Sprules Corporation

First published in 1994 by
Stoddart Publishing Co. Limited
34 Lesmill Road
Toronto, Canada
M3B 2T6
(416) 445-3333

A Boston Mills Press Book
The Boston Mills Press
132 Main Street
Erin, Ontario
N0B 1T0

Printed in Hong Kong

The publisher gratefully acknowledges the support of the Canada Council,
Ontario Ministry of Culture and Communications, Ontario Arts Council
and Ontario Publishing Centre in the development of writing and publishing in Canada.

FOREWORD

Every child who has been to a summer camp cherishes memories of those carefree days. The camps of Algonquin not only provide that irreplaceable experience, but also give many campers a special bonus—that opportunity to establish a personal bond with Algonquin Park.

"You are not only the owner of Camp Tanamakoon, you are also the guardian of a sacred trust. It is now your responsibility to preserve and maintain Tanamakoon for all of its past, present, and future campers." With these words, Carolea Butters, from whom I bought Camp Tanamakoon in 1984, passed on to me a message that she had received from her predecessors, Elizabeth and Ralph Raymer, who no doubt had received a similar message from Mary G. Hamilton, who had founded Tanamakoon in 1925. I am certain that all of the owners of the Algonquin camps received similar advice.

The owners and directors of the Algonquin Park camps have a strong commitment to their campers, a commitment to preserve and improve their camps. Each camp is immensely proud of its history and traditions. And each of us involved with these camps knows the role we play in developing that intimate relationship between the camper and the Park. It is our hope that every camper who reads this book will be able to rekindle that special connection that has meant so much to him or her. These pages preserve some of the sites, buildings, artifacts, traditions and beauty of Algonquin's summer camps. The words of Liz Lundell, the photographs of Bevereley Bailey, and the concept and design of John Taylor and Robbie Sprules have truly captured the uniqueness of the Algonquin camps.

It is also our sincere wish that these words and images will bring alive Algonquin and its summer camps for all readers, and that past and present campers may experience hours of enjoyment as they relive some of the best days of their lives, their days at Algonquin's great camps.

Kim Smith
Owner-Director
Camp Tanamakoon
February 1994

PREFACE

A book of this nature has lived in the hearts of the people who have known the wonderful Algonquin camps over many years. Their memories and dreams focus on the friendships and events that helped shape their lives at their camp, yet very few have had the opportunity to see any of the other camps that share a common history with their own.

For years, Robbie Sprules and John Taylor, of the international design firm Taylor/Sprules Corporation, have been frequent visitors to Algonquin Park. Robbie's father was a member of the original group of scientists who built and worked at the Harkness research lab on Lake Opeongo (where Robbie spent some of his summers), and his mother attended Wapomeo in the twenties. John's daughter attended Tanamakoon for years as a camper and is now spending the summer there as a C.I.T. At Tanamakoon, John and Robbie met Kim Smith, the camp's owner, and the three developed a friendship.

In the fall of 1992, Sprules and Taylor were once again in the Park—admiring the architecture of the camp buildings, the design details of the furniture, diverse graphic images of the camps, and the campers' signatures from years gone by. The dream of capturing the essence of summer camps in words and pictures began to take shape.

Kim Smith offered his support for the project and help in enlisting the other camp directors' assistance. Taylor/Sprules Corporation put together a plan for a rich and evocative visual interpretation of life at camp. The plan and the image were presented to General Publishing's Nelson Doucet and then to publisher John Denison at Boston Mills Press. Boston Mills Press contacted photographer Beverley Bailey, a former Swallowdale and Inawendawin camper, and also recruited writer Liz Lundell, who spent thirteen summers at Wapomeo as camper and staff. During a meeting at a Muskoka lodge, the idea took hold.

As Liz and Bev visited the eight camps, they were struck by the unique qualities of each, but also by the things the camps have in common. Each has its one-of-a-kind traditions and stories, but they are all participants in a larger camp experience. This book delights in the differences, but also celebrates the camps' collective participation in the whole wonderful experience that is summer camp.

Many other people lent their support as the project evolved. The camp directors, particularly Kim Smith, gave many hours of their time, and offered meals and accommodation. Their staff answered endless questions and ferried equipment in and around camp. The former directors and others who have lived in the Park also were generous with their time and camp knowledge. A few of the many deserve special thanks: Carolyn Beck; Ann Prewitt; Brookes Prewitt; Jim Spencer; Pam Thompson; Lee Warren; Mary Chestnut; Charles Geyer; Lance Kennedy; Richard Parker; Warren Prince; Mac Rand and Ann Shirrell; Margaret Roggow; Alex Thomson; Roy, Jeff and Mike Thrall; Gil and Conrad Yager; Judy Biggar; John Burry; Carol Devlin; Jack Eastaugh; Couchie Ebbs; Bill and Fran McColl; Dave Standfield; Don Standfield; Bill and Ellen Statten; Hugh Statten; Dr. Page Statten; Dr. Tay Statten; Taylor "Tike" Statten; Jill Vandal; Julie Wildman; Muriel Hall; Tom Hepburn; Larry Russe; Marilyn Smith; Patti Thom; Sue Thompson; Eugene Kates; Joanne Kates and Leon; Marc Rosenthal; David Bale; Max Bardenstein; Marilyn Mendelson; Vic Norris; the Perlmutters; David Stringer; and Idelle Trellay.

Don Burry generously shared his camp research, and Rory MacKay, Dan Strickland, and Pat and Ron Tozer helped with materials at the Algonquin Park Visitor Centre. Guy Burry provided his unceasing support. Editors Noel Hudson and Kathy Fraser applied their extensive expertise, and the translation of the text from camp vernacular reflects their patient efforts. In addition, Beverley thanks Gerry Segal, of Rainbow Camera, mentor and friend.

Initially, this book represented the vision of two people, but it has grown to mean much more. The dedication of the designers, editors, camp directors, and publisher shines through.

Finally, we would like to recognize the campers, past and present. Many still in camp, and others who found their way back to the Park in 1993, told their stories: some at the 80th reunion at Pathfinder, many at September Camp on Canoe Lake, a few who were visiting daughters at Northway, and others who are fortunate enough to be cottage leaseholders in Algonquin. For all of you who have experienced summer camp, and for those campers yet to come, we hope this book will serve as a record of Algonquin's great treasures and the most memorable aspects of a very special place—your camp.

L.L. B.B. J.T. R.S.

CAMPING COMES TO ALGONQUIN

THE EARLY DAYS OF CHILDREN'S CAMPING Amid soot and steam and the noisy chaos of the railway platform, mothers plant last, anxious kisses on their darlings. A handshake from Father, and youngsters hoist their backpacks and clamber up into the coach. Tiny faces press against the foggy glass as last waves are exchanged and then…all is motion. What a contrast when, nearly a day later, the young travellers disembark beside a calm, clear northern lake, bringing with them all of the plans they have dreamed of over the long winter spent in anticipation of the next few weeks—summer at camp in Algonquin Park.

The appearance of summer camps for children in North America coincided with increased industrialization and urban growth. The idea of a supervised program, far from the crime, smog, and unhealthy summer conditions of larger towns and cities, presented itself to a number of American educators

Arowhon campers arrive at Joe Lake Station, Algonquin Park, in the late 1940s.

and parents in the last half of the 1800s. Outdoor recreation was making its North American debut, and the thought of sending children off to spend a healthy summer engaged in outdoor pursuits appealed to many families of financial means. The first organized camping trips appeared during this period—many as summer extensions of boarding schools or military academies—and, by the turn of the century, hundreds of summer camps had been established in Maine, New Hampshire, Vermont, and other New England states.

The first organized children's camps in Canada were formed under the auspices of the Y. M. C. A. In 1891, Fraser Marshall founded the first: an Annual Boys' Encampment on a temporary site at Spencer's Point, Nova Scotia. Ontario Y camps followed. The first to have a permanent site, On-Da-Da-Waks, was established in 1896; it was later moved, under Wallace Forgie's directorship, to Golden Lake, 160 kilometres west of Ottawa.

Some American organizations sent canoe trips to Ontario's north woods. One of these was Camp Keewaydin, founded in Maine in 1893. Keewaydin set up a second camp, on Lake Temagami, in 1901. At the same time, A. L. Cochrane, a physical education instructor at Toronto's Upper Canada College, began leading groups of boys on canoe trips. In 1903, he settled on a Lake Temagami site, establishing the first private camp in Canada. Here the campers came in contact with the native people of Bear Island and a lasting link between "Indian lore" and organized camping was forged. At around the same time, improved rail transportation was beginning to open up other remote regions of Ontario, and one area that had increasing appeal was Algonquin.

ALGONQUIN PARK Algonquin Park was set aside in 1893 to preserve watersheds from deforestation, to provide a wildlife sanctuary, and to reserve in perpetuity a place for healthy recreation. The Park sits atop a highland dome, roughly 400 metres above sea level. The seven major rivers that have their headwaters here, and 1500 lakes, make it ideal canoe country. The western hills are clad in hardwoods: sugar maple, beech, and birch. The sandier eastern slopes are covered largely by stands of red,

white, and jack pine. Moose, deer, beaver, black bear, timber wolf, fisher, and marten live out their lives under the forest's cover, and the waters support brook trout, lake trout, smallmouth bass, as well as pike, muskellunge, and walleye in limited areas. Thousands of modern-day visitors come here each summer to see moose, listen for the wolf's wild call, or to delight in the loon's haunting song while slipping quietly over a calm lake on a sunset paddle.

Algonquin has witnessed many changes over its first century: the crosscut saw, shanty camps, and log drives have given way to modern timber harvesting; overtrapped animal populations have rebounded; luxurious wilderness hotels have come and gone; old farmsteads have been reclaimed by the forest. But Algonquin's appeal as a wilderness area for canoe trips and camping has remained a constant since the coming of the railway in 1896. City-weary tourists have long come to the Park to seek an invigorating or restful vacation in the north woods. As a 1928 Grand Trunk Railway brochure put it:

Deep within the hearts of most men and women slumbers an instinct as old as humanity itself. It is the desire to renew contact with Nature, to live and to play in Nature's solitudes and recesses. *It is the answer in man's soul to the lure of primeval spaces.*

In no other of Canada's famed playgrounds can man find more adequate answer to that desire than in Algonquin Park, vast forest and game reserve of 2721 square miles, gemmed with 1500 lakes of every conceivable size and shape, connected by a labyrinth of rivers and streams all unmarred by the inroads of exploitation and promotion.

Pioneers in the field of child development agreed with this ideal. Soon church groups, schools, and private educators began to look on Algonquin as an ideal setting for organized children's camping. In 1908, two American teachers led the way by selecting Cache Lake in Algonquin Park as the permanent home for two summer camps—Camp Waubuno for boys and Northway Lodge for girls.

"Typical trippers from Tanamakoon."

Learning to cook over a campfire.

OTHERS ALONG THE WAY In addition to the eight existing camps, several other youth programs have made Algonquin a summer home. Some private and public groups based elsewhere led canoe trips in the Park. There were also other residential camps that have since gone: Camp Waubuno at Cache Lake, established in 1908 by G. G. Bowers of Blair Academy, N.J.; Camp Ahmeek on Joe Lake, run by Albert Field of Columbus Academy, Ohio, from 1911-22; Camp Minne-wawa at Lake of Two Rivers, run by W. L. Wise of the Bordentown Military Institute, N.J., from 1911-30; Long Trail Camp on Joe Lake, just prior to World War I; Camp Ottertrail on Otter Slide Lake; Camp Douglas at Whitefish Lake, operated by Douglas Gardner from 1951-58; and Algonquin Experience Youth Camp on Whitefish Lake, which operated from 1974-82. In recent years, week-long space science programs for high-school students have been offered by Algonquin Space Campus at the radio telescope site on Lake Travers.

WHAT IS CAMP? Camp has meant a lot to the thousands of youngsters who have been to camp over the years, yet who ever really spelled out why it was so special when they were in the thick of the fun? We really only pause to reflect at special times—perhaps at the end of the session when we gather for misty-eyed replays of the challenges and triumphs of the summer, or years later, when we renew old friendships with camp buddies or return for a reunion to the place of so many happy memories.

Certainly the friendships are high on anyone's list of what makes camp special. As Charles Geyer, a Pathfinder alumnus, put it at his camp's eightieth reunion, "My first year at camp was 1934, and I couldn't wait to get up here in the summer. After bringing up my own kids, those were probably the happiest times of my life. You made a lot of lasting friends; Warren Prince is here for this reunion too, and he and I have been friends for more years than we'd like to remember."

"Algonquin Park is the most beautiful place on earth." —Michael, Camp Pathfinder

And then there are the traditions, the things that you can count on returning to year after year, whether it is the physical surroundings—some of the buildings have been in constant use since 1910—or the regular activities and events. Lee Warren came back to Camp Northway after an absence of thirty years to visit her daughter, Carly, who is now a counsellor. Lee says, "The wonderful thing is, that even though thirty years have gone by, it's just the same—it looks the same, they still sing the same songs, the language is the same, and the trips are the same. It's the only place in the world where, given the pace of change today, my daughter and I have the same experience. It's a wonderful connection." No matter how many times a family moved, or how many adjustments there were at home, camp remained a constant. That is why so many talk about camp as a second home, and about belonging to a big camp family.

The Algonquin camps share with other camps an emphasis on developing the individual child. Sometimes that entails learning new skills; achievement contributes to self-confidence. At other times, it is developing a sense of self-reliance and independence. Canoe trips are among the most significant experiences. Zach was on Tamakwa's thirteen-day trip to Algonquin's east side last summer. After descending the Petawawa River, the group had several days of difficult portaging through the centre of the Park to reach Opeongo Lake—including three portages over 4500 metres long. Fifteen-year-old Zach says, "I remember relishing the feeling, when we reached Happy Isle, that we'd accomplished the trip. When we paddled back into camp, it was a great feeling. For that moment, you're king of the world. You want to go back out." Camp helps you discover abilities you didn't know you had—physical, creative, and social.

P. R. Haywood's essay "What is Camping?" in a 1948 issue of *Canadian Camping* is still true today:

"Camp is what happens to the campers— What they take home in their memories"

We might say Camp is a "Place". We would covet for every camper, green woods, lakes, bird calls, quiet sunsets.... But, Camp is more than a "Place"....

We might say that a Camp is a "Plan". We would covet for every camper, a program which is thoroughly adapted to his or her needs at every step, which is not too crowded for comfort, yet which abounds in opportunities for zestful endeavour, all day long. Yet Camp is more than a "Plan"....

Camp is what happens to the Campers—what they take home with them in their memories, in their purpose, in their improved and newly acquired skills, in their friendships, in their appreciations.... That's what Camp is.

The Algonquin camps are all of this. They share an emphasis on tradition, on group living, and on developing the child, and they do this in one of the best settings for outdoor living that North America has to offer—Algonquin Park.

"*A green canoe and a paddle too.*" *A Tanamakoon trip, 1946.*

From Algonquin Park Canoe Routes map. A broken black line represents the old railway. Since 1959, campers have arrived via Highway 60.

EIGHT GREAT CAMPS

Eight residential children's camps are still going strong in Algonquin Park: Northway Lodge, founded in 1906; Camp Pathfinder, established on Source Lake in 1914; on Canoe Lake, Ahmek, founded in 1921, and Wapomeo in 1924; Tanamakoon, established on White's Lake (now Tanamakoon Lake) in 1925; Camp Arowhon on Buck (now Tepee) Lake, founded in 1934; Tamakwa, which opened on Tea Lake in 1937; and Wendigo, established on Cache Lake in 1965. Although the camps have many activities in common simply by their nature as summer camps and their common location, each is also unique.

When the first camps were created, the Park was recuperating from overtrapping, widespread logging, and devastating forest fires. Many of the present campsites were former logging camps or burned-out areas. Just after the turn of the century, leases were made available for cottages, hotels, and camps. The camps' founders were men and women of vision; they saw the potential for many happy, busy summers in spite of the deadfalls, tangled undergrowth, and stump-filled bays most encountered on their new leases.

In many ways, the individual character of each camp can be traced back to its early years. Ralph Waldo Emerson wrote, "Every institution is but the lengthened shadow of a man." Each camp, too, is a reflection of its founder's unique spirit.

"Camp's great 'cause you're so far from civilization." –Jeffrey, Camp Tamakwa

Land of the silver birch, Home of the beaver
Where still the mighty moose, Wanders at will.

Blue lake and rocky shore, I will return once more,
Boom de-de-boom, boom
Boom de-de-boom, boom
Boom de-de-boom, boom
Boom.

Northway Lodge

In 1906, Miss Fanny Case, a Rochester schoolteacher, took a group of her American students camping west of Algonquin Park, there initiating the first private camp for girls in Canada–Northway Lodge. Miss Case was a pioneer. She wanted to try informal education, away from the regimentation of regular classrooms. She wrote, "We were ripe for a break in the usual physical circumstances also accompanying education–close air, hard seats nailed down in rows, the clock ticking away our precious time and the bell cutting in just as an absorbed interest was reaching a climax." An outdoor setting allowed the girls to pursue individual interests unhampered by the constraints and conveniences of their city lives.

Two years later, Miss Case found a permanent site on Cache Lake in Algonquin Park. The property was on a sunny, south-facing point, but it was in rough condition; the second-growth brush was so thick that campers had to pick their way across the site by stepping on stumps and deadfalls.

From the beginning, the girls themselves did whatever site improvements were required; campers have had a hand in the construction of all of the permanent buildings at Northway. These early campers also selected the sites for platform tents, with views to the west so that the evening sun could warm them before it was time to turn in. Each tent was given a name, like Airy Bluff, Balsam Boughs, Birch Knoll–most of which are still in use today.

Miss Case was known for her genuine understanding of others, and often she dispensed with conventional approaches to form close, warmly supportive relationships with campers and staff. When one persistently difficult child was terrorizing her tent mates, Miss Case wondered aloud how helpful it might be if Janey were to spend some time

Fanny Case, a pioneer in camping, founded Northway Lodge for girls in 1906.

Everything at Northway preserves feelings of rustic simplicity and a closely knit family. The screened dining room looks out over the water.

The whole camp gathers at the point for games, skits, a campfire, and songs each evening.

lost in the woods. Somehow, the story is told, that circumstance came about, and Miss Case's simple solution worked wonders. In the days when all wore olive outfits on canoe trips, one camper wanted to wear red. Without saying no, Miss Case pointed out that the animals would be scared off, the guides might be disappointed at not seeing any wildlife, and rangers wouldn't recognize that this girl was from Northway and familiar with the woods. Of course, the red sweater disappeared. Dorothy Fergusson Foland wrote in a tribute to Fanny Case, "She had the rare gift of reaching out her hand and inviting you to do your thing, and showing where it would do the most good. She reached into us and pulled out the talents that others hadn't looked quite far enough to find."

Everything at Northway was designed to preserve a pioneering spirit; Miss Case wanted camp to be an adventure, a contrast to city life. Even today, there is no electricity, telephone, hot water, tape players, radios, or

Sizing up one of the newer canoes—a diminutive 9-foot cedar strip.

showers. Meals are cooked over a wood stove, well water is pumped by hand, and the girls take wash dips in the lake. There are no bells; the wake-up call is passed tent by tent down the line, and meals are announced by a song that crescendoes at an uncomfortable volume as each camper arrives and joins in: "Northway Lodge, Northway Lodge. Come together, come together. Girls! Girls! Girls! Girls! Lunch is ready. Lunch is ready."

Northway campers select their own activities and each girl has a canoeing counsellor she meets by appointment for individual instruction. As twelve-year-old Sarah explains, "You don't have to do anything here, but you're offered everything."

Northway campers feel they belong to one close camp family. Enrolment is capped at around fifty—half come from Canada and the other half come from several American states. Girls sit at whatever table they like in the dining hall. Canoe-trip groups deliberately mix campers from different tents, and every day the whole camp assembles at the point for Morning Council and for evening campfire.

Northway's unique character has been maintained with care over the years. Miss Case ran the camp until she was eighty. Ann Russe Prewitt, one of the founder's campers, then directed Northway for twenty-six years. After spending his young summers on Cache Lake, some as a Northway guide, Ann's son Brookes Prewitt took over seventeen years ago. Brookes has consciously preserved Northway's rustic traditions, and the camp is still as close to a wilderness experience as any residential camp can be. As C. F. Plewman once wrote, "To some, Camp Northway might seem severe; to others, a chance to recapture reality."

Fanny L. Case

Look close upon the shore
The tiny Sun-dew glistens in the early light
Beside a weathered tent a grey pre-cambrian
Rock stands watch—settled and silent—
A shawl of moss thick grown upon its ancient back
High on a fragile limb, the sparrow sings
"Sweet Canada, Canada, Canada."

Where is the heart that once led children here?
Where is the one who broke each child away from
patterned, static life and taught
Each eye to see, each hand to give, each soul to love?
Where is Miss Case who showed all how to
Sing their lives in blended harmony?
Where is she now?

Look close upon the shore
The tiny Sun-dew glistens in the early light
Beside a weathered tent a grey pre-cambrian
Rock stands watch—settled and silent—
A shawl of moss thick grown upon its ancient back
High on a fragile limb, the sparrow sings
"Sweet Canada, Canada, Canada."

Ann Prewitt
14 August, 1960
Camp Chat (Northway annual)

20

The campers sit wherever they choose in the dining hall.

The dining hall was built in 1908, although its roof was canvas then. Campers are surprised at breakfast with invitations to go on trip.

PATHFINDER

Camp Pathfinder's island campsite is cloaked in cedar, red pine, and well-aged birch. The root-laced paths wind under close tree cover from the dining hall, past the line of tents—Cree Row, Skid Row, Luigiville—to the chapel and council ring beyond. Franklin Gray, originally from Barrie, Ontario, was a physical education teacher in Rochester when he and his partner established Camp Pathfinder in 1914. Today it is the longest running boys' camp in Algonquin.

Gray felt the Source Lake location was ideal; there was good rail access, it was in an excellent spot to strike out for canoe trips, yet it was fairly removed from other settlement in the Park. When Gray's partner, Mr. Bennett, withdrew for health reasons in 1917, Herman Norton, another Rochester physical education teacher, became involved, and he ran the camp as sole director from 1925.

"I want to tramp on o'er those blazed trails with my tump line on my head..."

When Pathfinder alumni talk about the early days at camp, the imposing presence of Chief Norton looms large. Under his leadership, the camp had something of the air of a military school. He would tour the island regularly, noting in a little black book any sloppiness or items that required repair, then he would direct one of his lieutenants to rectify the situation. His most quoted saying was "Organization, deputization, and supervision."

One of the many activities Chief Norton initiated was the study of Indian lore. The campers worked their way up through three levels: Tall Pine, Central Fire, and Medewiwin. Dan "Lance" Kennedy, assistant director, remembers the final test required to achieve the highest

"We're wild! We're woolly! We're rough like a saw! Pathfinder! Pathfinder! Raw! Raw! Raw!"

The Pathfinder Candy Store was the original Source Lake Station building. It was moved to the island after passenger service ceased in 1959.

rank; he completed a solo vigil on the other side of the lake to join the select circle of the Medewiwin. The old council ring, another product of Chief Norton's interest in Indian lore, still stands, tucked into the trees behind the baseball diamond. At the head of the ring is a log structure carved with totems and native symbols; beneath the central figure of the eagle sat the Chief.

The ring is quiet now and the weekly councils have moved, but the Chief's log cabin with its stone fireplace is still the director's cabin. Reveille and taps are still played on the bugle, as they were in his day, and the regular council fires, where the headman from each trip presents a report, continue at a larger venue that everyone still refers to as the new council ring, even though it has been there since the early thirties.

Bill Swift and Roy Thrall took over ownership from the Chief in the early sixties, and, at age seventy-five, Roy still returns each summer. Mac Rand has been directing the camp since 1982. All three are former campers and staffmen. Mac's father was also at Pathfinder; he was part of the group that brought boatloads of Michigan clay over from the train stop to build the tennis court.

Chalked on a beam in the lower office alongside Mac's entry are his father's and brother's scrawl: Stan Rand 27-37 and Mike Digger Rand 59, 64-68. As Mac says of the directorship, "We've kept it in the Pathfinder family."

The focus at Pathfinder has always been more on canoe-tripping than on in-camp activities. The Chief used to appeal to the boys' sense of adventure when he conducted his promotional tours in Buffalo, Rochester, and other New York communities. His brochures incorporated a special appeal to prospective campers:

Chief Norton's love of native lore gave the camp its Indian councils.

A Message to Boys

Have you ever hiked through virgin forests, paddled through mountain lakes and streams, matched your skill with a gamey trout, and at the end of a day's paddling and hiking, pitched your tent on some rugged spot and cooked and eaten your supper amidst the pines, cedars and balsams of the Canadian Woods?...If you haven't, you have missed a thrill of your life time. If you have, you will feel the call to try it again. Pathfinder provides these thrills and many others.

externally recognized awards. The same is true of other activities; campers pursue them out of interest or for pleasure rather than to earn awards. The only formal recognition of ability is a Pathfinder certificate noting Above Average achievement.

There have been roughly a hundred campers each half in the past few years, mostly from Buffalo, New York, and Toronto. Of the fifty staffmen in 1993, only four were new to the camp. Year after year, Pathfinder ways have been handed down: where to find the best campsites, how to tie a tump line on a canoe, why campers paddle on one side and the sternsman on the other. As Mac Rand tells a group of boys the night before they head out on trip, "You guys are carrying on something that's been going on for a very long time."

Pathfinder campers still live under canvas in platform tents and only a few of the larger buildings have electricity. Campers go out on several canoe trips each session; the most exciting have been two trips to James Bay, one in 1986 and the other in 1993. Although swimming staff provide instruction, the boys have little time in camp to work on any

"Some most enjoyable times were my seven years here." G. Yager

The bugle call that heralds the start of the day is heard down the tent line.

AHMEK

When Taylor Statten opened Camp Ahmek in 1921, he had already been involved in boys' work for nineteen years with the Y. M. C. A. Statten joined the Y in 1902 because of his interest in youth leadership as much as for the religious aspects. In 1905, he took a full-time position with the organization, and he also took on the directorship of their Camp Couchiching that summer. There he became known as the Chief because he enlivened the Christian program with Indian lore and woodcraft each summer.

Statten first brought his family to Canoe Lake on a canoe trip in 1913; he took out a lease for a summer home on what is now Little Wapomeo Island after that visit. The Stattens spent the first year in a teepee his wife, Ethel, had made, but a permanent cottage followed in 1915. Their friend George Chubb, Statten's business manager at Ahmek for thirty-eight years, designed the stone fireplace; Tom Thomson assisted in construction, procuring sand for the mortar from nearby Sims Pits. The message carved into that mantelpiece has become an informal maxim at Ahmek: "Here Let the Northwoods Spirit Kindle Fires of Friendship."

In the summer of 1920, Statten ran a leadership camp at Canoe Lake, and the following summer he opened Camp Ahmek—the first Canadian-owned private camp in Algonquin. The name came from the Algonquian word for beaver, and Statten was dubbed by his friend James Edmund Jones, Gitchiahmek, Great Beaver in Ojibwa. The main camp stretched along the sandy beach at the northeast end of Canoe Lake and the boys lived in tents those first years.

Taylor was an inspirational speaker who had a showman's flair. In *The Y. M. C. A. in Canada,* Murray G. Ross described Taylor.

The Seton cabin and totem pole entrance to the old council ring. Early 1920s.

"When we get up to Ahmek, what a riot we will make...." The Ahmek canoe docks, the swim docks, and the dining hall behind.

He was able:

to unify and simplify objectives, to dramatize them and to rally existing resources around their service. Possessed of great zeal, imagination, and vision, he had the 'spark of the prophet' which stirred others and won them to the cause he was advancing.

Harry Ebbs, who later married the Stattens' daughter, Couchie, also described the Chief's charismatic effect on audiences:

In 1922, there was a father and son banquet in Peterborough and he came through for the Y. M. C. A. It was a full house. He just had everybody spellbound; it was a very inspirational thing. It hit me as a young fellow and...that was how eventually I got up to Ahmek as a counsellor.

Taylor Statten's grandfather's cousin was showman Phineas Taylor (P.T.) Barnum, and the Chief seems to have inherited his great-uncle's love of pageantry. During winter months in the city, Statten would often dress up in a beaded deerskin outfit with feather headdress and stage mini council rings to promote Ahmek.

Camping in Canada was largely untried ground at the time Ahmek started, and the Chief was willing to test new ideas, although many had to be discarded later. One such idea was the award shields. Each boy received cast-iron bars to tack onto an oak shield, denoting the skill levels he had attained that summer. There were bars for boxing, campcraft, trees, citizenship, and astronomy, besides the regular camp activities. By the late twenties, however, it seemed that collecting the awards was detracting from the true purpose of camp, so the shields were abandoned. Cups and trophies, donated by parents, went the same way; barrels full of tarnished silverware collected in the storehouse.

The Chief was largely a self-educated man, and he had a great sense of curiosity. He loved the limelight, but knew enough to surround himself with other skilled people and had a knack for attracting those he thought could offer something interesting to campers. For

Painted to honour the Chief's 25th year in camping. J.E.Sampson–1930.

30

example, the music staff included people such as Mario Bernardi, Murray Adaskin, and Sir Ernest MacMillan. In 1922, Ernest Thompson Seton brought his understanding of campcraft and native lore to Ahmek; Indian council rings have been a feature there ever since. Champion diver Dick Van Valkenburg taught aquatics in the first years. Several experts from the nearby Golden Lake First Nation also contributed over the years. Bill Stoqua, an Algonquin guide, taught canoeing, and his technique was adopted as the Ahmek paddling style. During the twenties and thirties, Matt Bernard had an "Indian village" on Wigwam Bay, close to main camp, where he built birchbark canoes and demonstrated other crafts. Basil Partridge, known at camp as Anishanabe, taught campcraft, and he also built the log Bay Cabin in the late forties. Jack Miner and Stuart Thompson were among visiting naturalists, and ranger Mark Robinson regaled campers with stories about wildlife and Park history.

Dining hall plaques by Jack Eastaugh depict camp history. The pirate ship, 1925.

The Chief always felt there was good to be found in every boy when properly challenged. He believed that by assuming increasing responsibility boys would shine. Many of his morning talks or meditations were about self-improvement and rising to a challenge, or about doing good by putting the other guy first. This notion is still referred to as the Ahmek Spirit.

Ahmek grew rapidly. The first summer there were 30 campers; by 1929, there were 250. Enrolment peaked at over 300 in the early eighties, but it is back to a more comfortable total of roughly 225 for each month. Twenty percent of the campers come from Québec, slightly over half of the campers come from Ontario and other parts of Canada, 15 percent are from the United States, and 10 percent come from other countries, including Mexico, Europe, and Australia.

Because of Ahmek's size, the boys are divided into five sections by age group. Each section operates almost as a miniature camp, attending activities and planning evening programs independently. The campsite has expanded over the years to take in piney slopes to the east, where the twelve- to fourteen-year-olds now live, and a slightly removed area to the west of Ghost Walk Creek, home of the senior boys since 1947. Campers frequently paddle from section to section.

Out of all of the activities at Ahmek, the program that has grown the most is canoe-tripping. Campers can now sign up for trips to the Temagami, Kipawa, Killarney, Quetico, and Biscotasing areas, some up to fifty days long, in addition to regular Park trips.

Ahmek's directorship has stayed in the family for three generations. After rising through the ranks as camper and staff, "Dr. Tay," the Chief's son, gradually took over the full operation of the camp from his father in the fifties. His other son, Page, also occupied a number of positions on summer staff, and ran the September Camp for alumni and families. Today, Taylor "Tike" Statten III is director.

Over the years, thousands of young lives have been influenced by Camp Ahmek and, through it, by Taylor Statten. When they congregate in the dining hall, the boys can still look up to the Chief, to where his portrait hangs in a place of honour above the fireplace.

Spirit of Ahmek

Lift we our hearts to the home of our dream,
Where beauty of Nature and sky's glory gleam.
Deep in the wildwood set like a gem,
Hail to old Ahmek, the maker of men.
Here broods the spirit of life of the age.
Here calls the future for saviour and sage.
Pledge we our hearts to thy spirit again,
Spirit of Ahmek, the maker of men.

Music: Sir Ernest MacMillan

Lyrics: Dr. Eustace Haydon

A stiff breeze propels surfers toward the Voyageur section.

Voyageurs, Mountaineers, and Pioneers cross Wigwam Bay Bridge on their way to main camp.

WAPOMEO

Wapomeo was formed as Ahmek's sister camp in 1924. The eldest of the Stattens' three children is nicknamed Couchie; when Taylor and Ethel brought their twelve-day-old baby girl to Camp Couchiching for the summer of 1909, the campers there nicknamed her after the lake. They thought her real name, Adele, was "a bit sissy." After Ahmek was created, Couchie expressed an interest in going to camp. All of her friends were at Glen Bernard, just west of the Park, but Taylor decided to start his own girls' camp.

Ethel Statten was to be director. She was known at camp as Tonakela, which in Ojibwa means, "you first." The Stattens had a lease on South Tea Lake that the Chief recommended for a site, but Tonakela objected. Couchie recalls her mother's words: "No way will I have a girls' camp away from Ahmek." So it was decided that Wapomeo's first home would be on the family's island, thereafter

"Here Let the Northwoods Spirit Kindle Fires of Friendship." At Little Wapomeo.

called Little Wap, as campers and staff abbreviate the name. With that, all of Ahmek's board of directors resigned, insisting that parents would be scandalized at the thought of boys and girls sharing the same lake. As it turned out, many parents with sons at Ahmek endorsed the plan for their daughters; it was more convenient to deal with one business office for both camps; brothers and sisters were brought together each Sunday; and visiting was made easier with all children on the same lake.

The Stattens' friend James Edmund Jones again supplied a name—Wapomeo—which meant "bluebirds of happiness." The camp colours of green and grey came from a Rose Fyleman poem: "I know an island in the lake, green upon waters grey..." The Statten's own cottage was Wapomeo's main lodge, and the youngest campers slept upstairs. With space at a premium, the others slept in

The Wapomeo dining hall, first built in 1928, but enlarged substantially in recent years. The light shades were woven by craftspeople at the C.N.I.B.

four double-deckers; these were two-storey structures with camper cabins flanking the counsellors' accommodation. The girls had their own council ring and a platform for modern dance on the island. The Wapomeo horses and a herd of cows for fresh milk were on the mainland, at Mowat.

In 1928, things had become so cramped at Little Wap that the senior girls moved to a much larger island a kilometre to the south, where they had their own dining hall and a separate program. In 1932, to reduce costs during the Depression, it became necessary to amalgamate the kitchens. All of the girls moved to Big Wap, leaving the cottage to the Stattens once again. The former dining hall was dragged over the ice, and today it houses arts and crafts on Wapomeo's Main Island. The older girls moved again, after World War II, to another island to the east of Main Island.

One of two 42-foot Peterborough canoes custom built for Taylor Statten in 1925.

Wapomeo had some of the same organizational aspects as Ahmek. The central unit at Wap was also the cabin group. The reasoning behind separate staff quarters was that the six campers in each cabin would have a chance to sort out dynamics independently, and work on co-operation, self-discipline, and other group skills. The girls were also divided into sections by age. Some other plans initiated at Ahmek, such as morning meditations and the award shields, were adopted, however, Wapomeo really operated independently, developing its own activities and unique personality.

Couchie led one of the first canoe trips, two weeks across the north end of the Park, when Mark Robinson was the ranger at Cedar Lake. Says Couchie, "He was struck dumb when he tried to pick up our packs. He said, 'These are far too heavy for ladies to carry.'" As Couchie took on more and more of the directorship, she always let prospective staff know that "every counsellor took out her own cabin group trip. So if she didn't like trip, she didn't come."

Over the years, Wapomeo campers have filled their busy days with pottery, nature lore, archery, show nights in the lodge, riding, tennis, weaving, and crafts, in addition to all the waterfront activities. In the early years, the campers did Morning Jerks to warm up before skinny dips. A curtain was drawn across the swim docks to provide privacy from boat traffic. Another ongoing interest is music. The girls continue to sing about their camp–on trip, while paddling to meals or activities, and in the cabin, as in this favourite song:

There's an island somewhere
Where we can get away
From the bustling city
And all the weary days.
We will leave our homes
each summer
To join our friends once more
On that happy wooded isle,
Canoe Lake shore.

"You get the feeling and you know it's there, bonds of friendship everywhere."

Past and present Wapomeo campers remember sitting with counsellor and cabin group in the dining hall, the open stone hearth at its centre, voices joined in harmony rising to the rafters, where a very special canoe hangs. The canoe is inscribed with the date July 7, 1921; it was presented to Couchie after she swam from Little Wap to Ahmek on her twelfth birthday.

Couchie was Wapomeo's director from 1930 to 1975. Tike Statten took over from her for the next twelve years. Today, Jill Vandal is in charge of the roughly 240 campers who come to stay each month. Echoing what previous Wapomeo campers have felt, campers Zaira, Isabela, Ashley, and Dayne listed the best things about their 1993 summer at camp: "The activities, meeting new people, the friends, our counsellor.... The canoe trip was wicked, too."

Each morning, Wapomeo campers gather on the Main Island swim docks. They recite the Sanskrit verse that has provided inspiration here and at other camps. The familiar words have formed a lasting memory for three generations of girls, and often gain even more meaning in later life when campers reminisce about their Wapomeo days:

> *Listen to the Salutation to the Dawn.*
> *Look to this day for it is life,*
> *The very life of life.*
> *In its brief course lie all the*
> *verities and realities of our existence:*
> *The glory of action,*
> *The bliss of growth,*
> *The splendour of beauty.*
> *For yesterday is but a dream*
> *and tomorrow is only a vision,*
> *But today well spent, makes every yesterday*
> *a dream of happiness and every tomorrow a*
> *vision of hope.*
> *Look well, therefore, to this day.*

"Daughters of Canoe Lake Moon" –Council Ring fire dancers.

The view from the pottery shop. Senior Island (far shore) is a short paddle from Main Wap's canoe docks.

TANAMAKOON

Old girls often remark on how little has changed at Camp Tanamakoon since Mary G. Hamilton was director. Mary G, as she was affectionately called, was a physical education teacher at Toronto's Margaret Eaton School when she started the camp in 1925. The school was primarily involved in training physed. and literature teachers, and Miss Hamilton needed a setting where her students could be trained in camping leadership and outdoor recreation. She was also interested in starting a summer camp for girls.

The site, on what was originally called White's Lake, had been burned thirteen years earlier in a forest fire. Despite the scrubby growth, the spot had many attractions. One point faced the sunrise, another fronted a shallow bay—ideal for swimming and canoeing. Just a short trip east, across the narrow lake and beyond a stretch of river, was Cache Lake, with the Highland Inn, Algonquin Park Headquarters, and most importantly, Algonquin Park Station.

Miss Hamilton narrowed the choice of names to two: Tanamakoon, which translates as "Hail fellow, well met," or Dawandena, "Dawn of the day." She chose Tanamakoon. The eastern point, where a council ring was constructed a short time later, was named Dawandena. Girls often take a few quiet moments there, sitting on the sloping rock that overlooks the eastern side of the lake.

The cabins and tents stretch along the shore, and the communal buildings sit back on higher ground. From the east, first come the Algonquin tents. Next are the Sioux and Ojibway cabins. The swim docks jut out from the point that separates those younger campers from the Shawnees, and finally the oldest girls, the Crees.

At Woodcraft. Each bead on the centennial necklaces represents a different camp.

A Worthy Woodsman candidate presents her nature talk at morning assembly in the lodge. The bronze batchets, with recipients' names, are on the right wall.

Twigs on a golden pine board spell out the welcome to Tanamakoon. Flights of granite steps rise between low stone retaining walls from the swim docks to the lodge. The flagpole stands at the second level, where the pines that were just saplings in 1925 have grown tall. Farther up is Mary G's old cabin; known as Waubanoose for many years, it is now called Hamilton Hall in her honour.

The lodge was one of the first buildings; it originally housed the kitchen, dining room, and recreation room. Full-camp assemblies are still held here every morning. The wrought-iron candelabra in the shape of pine trees and the well-worn wicker chairs for the counsellors are still here—the lodge holds a special place in the memories of all Tanamakoon girls.

The campers have always been divided into tribes by age, although new sections had to be added as numbers grew. Today, roughly 170 girls attend for two weeks or a month, and each of the

tribes elects a Little Chief, a camper representative meets regularly with the staff Tribal Head.

Tanamakoon is the only Algonquin camp where campers wear a uniform. In the early days, the counsellors wore light green bloomers and middies, while the campers wore khaki—even on trip. Mary Hamilton described in her book, *The Call of Algonquin*, a guide's last-minute instructions to his charges: "We're getting near camp now; roll up your socks and spit out your gum." Bloomers have given way to shorts, and campers now wear tan T-shirts, but the distinction of the green shirt for staff is preserved to this day.

The camp crest features a fawn. Up until the late sixties, white-tailed deer were abundant in the Park, especially wherever new tree growth made foraging easier. The Park superintendent's daughter came to camp one of the first summers, and brought Flag, a five-week-old orphan deer who became Tanamakoon's mascot and permanent emblem.

Campers look for aunts' and mothers' names on posts that date back to 1953.

The program has seen a few changes. Riding was abandoned in 1948, once it became increasingly difficult to reach the trails, because campers had to cross Highway 60, built through the southeastern part of the Park during the 1930s. The horse barn became the home of the arts and crafts program. Sailing races with Northway Lodge also disappeared, but more things have remained the same than have changed. Music and theatre have always been an important part of life at Tanamakoon, and on Sunday evenings the girls still congregate in the lodge for music night. The campers still wear bathing caps marked with their names and colour-keyed to their swimming ability. Campcraft remains one of the most popular activities; the highest honour at the camp remains the Worthy Woodsman award.

Mary Hamilton believed in leadership training, and a lasting manifestation of that is the contribution each tribe is expected to make

The sign post, started in 1940 with mileage to war guests' homes.

to the camp's smooth operation. The youngest girls are responsible for cleaning up outside their cabins, while the oldest, the Crees, arrange and lead games for the junior campers. Swim biscuits—the after-swim crackers with peanut butter—are prepared and distributed by campers each day on a rotating basis. The Crees once summarized the camp's aims, and their verse hangs in the lodge:

We Aim

To live out the things we believe
To have a sincere care for all people,
To be disciplined in all we do,
To see the job that needs to be done
and carry it through,
To be constructive in our
thinking and speaking,
To learn to work in a group,
To be willing to recognize and
correct our faults,
To study and work for sound homes, united
communities and a peaceful world.

In 1953, Mary Hamilton sold the camp to a former camper and her husband, Elizabeth and Ralph Raymer. After the Raymers, another Tanamakoon girl took over; Carolea Butters and her husband, Hugh, ran the camp from 1974-83. The present owners are Kim and Marilyn Smith. Most of the program is run just as it was in Miss Hamilton's day, and Kim gives a good summary of the camp's continuing goals: "Tanamakoon is a piece of a solid foundation of a person's youth–a place that tries to hang on to what it is by design, so girls can feel happy, safe, and comfortable here year after year."

The camp co-director is Patti Thom, who celebrated her thirtieth summer at Tanamakoon in 1993. Mary Hamilton returned to the camp for just one visit, shortly before she died in 1972. Patti was one of the young campers who assembled on the lodge steps to sing the founder her favourite Tanamakoon song:

Oh, Algonquin, I'll return some day to these wilds

And take pack and paddle in my hand

My paddle will sing a song across the waters

And my feet will pound a path upon the hills.

TANAMAKOON

1925

Cree Flats and the Sun Life Building—a composting toilet.

The older Crees aspire to spending their last summer as campers in Cabin A. They leave their "tradition" painted on the wall at the month's end.

AROWHON

The central structure at Camp Arowhon is a large log building called the main lodge. From its steps, you can look out over Tepee Lake. You see boys and girls sprinting along to activities; a couple of campers wrestle on the large lawn around the flagpole. Off to the left, beyond the windsurfing area, come cheers from the girls' swim dock. Mainsails snap at the sailing docks where campers are rigging the Snipes. Farther right, and just out of view along a wide sandy path, is the canoe dock. Beyond that a white birch tree marks the boundary of the exclusive domain of the oldest boys–The Point. Small wonder that Camp Arowhon is described as a busy waterfront camp.

The main lodge, like the other log structures around camp, has an interesting past. In 1931, Ernest Thompson Seton and Ellsworth Jaeger opened an adult camp called Camp of the Red Gods on

Early Arowhon campers learning how to finish their own paddles.

this site. Red Gods went bankrupt the following year, leaving a number of these log buildings and an ideal site for a children's camp.

At the time, Lillian Kates was the wife of a Toronto dentist whose business was also feeling the effects of the Depression. Lillian decided to start a children's camp to meet the family's expenses and save their home. She heard that the Red Gods lease was available and she approached the appropriate bureaucrat, who promptly refused her offer. Lillian proposed that if she could get 80 percent of the Red Gods creditors to settle with her, the lease would be signed over. Never believing this feisty immigrant could manage it, the official agreed.

There were no phones in the Park then and the highway didn't exist. Lillian Kates hired locals to paddle her in to meet carpenters, masons, and lumbermen. Most of the tradesmen were so

Arowhon's main lodge was one of many buildings left by the Camp of the Red Gods. Lillian Kates bought the lease during the Depression.

"United we stand, divided we fall. We're all for one and one for all. And we can't stop loving our Arowhon." Tuck line at the main lodge.

happy to get even the smallest payment that they signed agreements accepting seven to twelve cents on the dollar. Lillian returned to Toronto to claim the lease. According to her granddaughter, Joanne Kates, "The bureaucrat turned white and blue, and gasped for air...but the lease was hers."

Next Lillian got out a map. She put the point of a compass on Algonquin Park and drew a circle around the area that was within one day's drive. Armed with Temple Sisterhood directories for those cities, she set out for Cincinnati, Buffalo, Detroit, and New York, where she telephoned complete strangers to convince them to send their children to Camp Arowhon. She decided the camp should be co-educational, so that if there were a boy and a girl in a family, both could come. Granny Kates opened Arowhon the summer of 1934, in the depths of the Depression, as the first co-ed camp in Algonquin. As her granddaughter Joanne summarizes, "The words 'I can't' were not in her vocabulary."

The original camp crest was a large yellow A, with a Hollywood-style spear-bearing Indian in full headdress at the centre. It came to symbolize the romance of the wilds, and, at the same time, preserved the camp's previous connection with the Red Gods. The camp's name was another hybrid—a blend of arrows and Samuel Butler's utopian novel, *Erewhon*.

Mrs. Kates' son Eugene was her right-hand man during her directorship. In 1939, she took another lease around the corner on Little Joe Lake and built a lodge to house visiting parents. Arowhon Pines became a successful resort, taking increasing amounts of her time. She left the camp to Eugene's sole direction when he returned after the war. Since 1990, Eugene's daughter Joanne (known for her work as a restaurant critic and journalist) has been running camp, making Arowhon and the Taylor Statten camps the only Algonquin camps run by the same family for three generations. Although he now spends most of his time running Arowhon Pines, Eugene still has his cabin at camp, and his granddaughter is now a camper. Joanne says, "I expect to run camp until my daughter or son take it over."

The camp looks almost as it did in the days when Lillian ran it, and there continues to be an emphasis on individualized instruction. Eugene explains: "The value of the camp experience is almost directly proportionate to the number of skills a child learns. It's important to let people learn the feeling of doing something well. The kids bloom if you can get them hooked on striving for excellence, and that's what I think a camp should do."

Each of the roughly two hundred campers chooses his or her individual program every day, from riding, drama, arts and crafts, tennis, archery, land sports, kayaking, and other water activities.

About a third of the present campers are second generation, and there are grandchildren here, too. Chucky, a seasoned camper, says, "Camp is great. I can get rid of my parents for two months, and the first day back at camp is so special because you get to see everyone again." Fellow camper Myles agrees, "Camp is like a dream compared to the city." Regular high jinks include shaving cream raids on other sections and skits at every meal. Mealtimes are noisy times, with occasional food fights and raucous singing, and Joanne joins in with gusto. "When my daughter was born I taught her camp songs before I taught her important words, so she could sing Camp Arowhon 'Junior Liberation' when she was two.... Camp is the only place in the world where it doesn't matter if you carry a tune, you're still welcome to sing," she said in a CBC radio interview.

Like several other camps today, Arowhon places more emphasis on nurturing kids and developing relationships, but camp is pretty much the same. The biggest change—and one that has drawn mixed reactions—is a facelift for the Arowhon crest. Joanne has substituted a graphic design at the centre of the A, because she felt uncomfortable with the cultural appropriation and stereotyping in the old one. Some campers, past and present, were upset, proving that even a small change can draw passionate reactions when you're messing with a cherished camp tradition.

Camp Arowhon we always will remember
The bond of friendship that we have designed.
Each memory will be a burning ember,
That will live in each heart and soul and mind.
Through the years our friends will linger here beside us,
Sharing joys and sorrows through the years.
We will always have our comradeship to guide us,
And the moments we love and hold so dear.

One for each person, 400 flames flicker during candlelighting.

Over sixty canoes are ready for paddlers. Lorne Greene designed the Rec. Hall (left); the old boathouse is an original Red Gods building.

TAMAKWA

When a visitor arrives at Camp Tamakwa, there's an all-camp welcome in the dining hall. The two hundred campers sing loudly, "We welcome, we welcome you." Then each of the six sections breaks into their section cheer—stamping on the floor, thumping on tables and generally trying to outshout each other. It is a genuinely warm, if close to deafening, initiation into the Tamakwa family.

If you look around the dining hall once the noisy crowd has burst out the doors on their way to activities, you will find silent recognition of Tamakwa's founders everywhere. On the pine walls are black-and-white photos of the early years. Here is Lou Handler, the Detroit Forestry graduate turned professional boxer and coach, demonstrating how to make a balsam bed. Close by is a shot of Lou paddling with Omer Stringer, canoeing legend and

"Unca" Lou, forestry graduate and boxer, loved both the woods and kids.

woodsman. And on the east wall is a touching tribute a young camper crafted all on his own: a green board lovingly lettered in shaky white capitals, "In Memory of "Unca" Lou Handler." Below is a small snapshot of Lou. Above it reads the Hebrew verse, "Behold how good and pleasant it is for brothers and sisters to dwell together in harmony."

Lou Handler was a counsellor at Camp Arowhon in 1936 when he first met Omer Stringer. Omer, who was born just outside the Park, was teaching his famed canoeing technique at camps. He was paddling toward the dock at full tilt that day, and Lou braced for a crash. With one of his seemingly effortless manoeuvres, Omer brought the canoe to an impressive stop right at Lou's feet. Omer's son, David Stringer, describes Tamakwa's beginnings: Although Lou had a Forestry degree "this was his first dose of wilderness reality up

"Tamakwa, Tamakwa, what a wonderful spot. What a lodge, what a camp, what a place." The lone pine (bottom right) is a welcoming landmark.

here. Lou was smitten, so much so, that he wanted to start a camp." Omer knew the Park well and had a full repertoire of practical skills. That fall they searched for a site. They originally selected Smoke Lake, but Nominigan—an outpost of the Highland Inn—was already operating there, and the authorities objected to two commercial enterprises on one lake. The Stattens, however, were willing to sell the lease initially intended for Wapomeo on South Tea Lake.

The Tamakwa legend describes the two men paddling up to the campsite on a crisp fall day in 1936. They scrambled up a pine-clad slope to the sandy, south-facing point, looked over Tea Lake and realized this would be the future home of Camp Tamakwa. A more accurate picture shows the shallow bay to the left filled with stumps, and the main camp area a tangle of brush, but the decision was made. At first, the 5-acre lease stretched from Voyageur Point in the west to the boathouses. In 1949, after another 5 acres were acquired, a girls' section was added, and the camp reached its present size.

Today's campers are split equally between Americans and Canadians.

The first winter, Omer and his two brothers lived in a tent while they built the original log structures. The present doctor's residence was one of the first. Omer also designed the camp logo of a beaver felling a tree; Tamakwa comes from the Algonquian phrase "beaver chewing wood." The first brochure advertised "The Algonquin Park Camp for Boys," quoting Longfellow's lines, "This is the forest primeval. The murmuring pines and the hemlocks..." Twenty-seven boys signed up for that first summer of 1937.

Lou wanted to share his love of nature with campers. Max Bardenstein, who has been on Tea Lake since he first came to Tamakwa in 1947, described Lou: "He was very human. Here was this six-foot-four, two-hundred-and-thirty-pound ex-boxer who had the ability to give love unconditionally to a lot of young people." Citing an example of "Unca" Lou's magic, Max spoke about a young boy who, in spite of the staff's efforts, was left out of everything because he was a non-swimmer. Lou took him aside and spent time with him on boxing. When the boy won a match, he became a camp hero. Within the month, his whole outlook had changed and he was able to swim just over a kilometre to Treasure Island. "That's the kind of thing Lou would do," says Max. "He was the centre of something very good." No one can confirm where the name Unca came from. It might be a diminutive "uncle" or a title he received from a native band, but it embodied the affection campers and staff felt for their gentle leader.

Omer Stringer was always at camp in the summer to teach canoeing and campcraft. Lou's sister Esta and her husband, Mike Kraft, were also well-loved regulars at camp. Lou Handler died in 1974, but former campers and staff David Bale, Vic Norris, and Howard Perlmutter bought the camp from Lou and Esta's estate in 1981.

Some activities have changed since Lou's day. Horseback riding has gone. For a time, waterskiing was a big attraction, but it has recently been banned in Algonquin to enhance the natural character of the Park. Half-court tennis has been added, and so have kayaking and a ropes course. David Stringer believes his father would be happy with Tamakwa today, watching kids pursue activities that are in tune with the Algonquin environment. "If he could see this third generation of kids tipped over on the side of their canoe, paddling, he'd be thrilled."

The camp now has two offices: one in Detroit and one in Toronto, and enrolment is split equally between American and Canadian campers. Vic's task is attracting the Michigan kids, who could choose from many camps closer to home. Algonquin Park and the canoe trips are the drawing cards. He stresses the pristine beauty and the opportunities of the setting; there are no other cottages on the lake, and the site is accessible by boat only. He finds that Algonquin is "a place that even the youngest kids find inspirational, and it's the kind of exposure that stays with them for the rest of their lives."

Every day after rest hour, campers get a snack of fresh fruit — Tootsie Frootsie.

55

One place that is most special to Tamakwans is the Slope—a set of steps that reaches about 30 feet from the plateau of main camp down to the lake. At the foot of the Slope is a platform with a fireplace and Unca Lou's chair. The camp family congregates here every Friday night for a non-religious service, and the first one of every summer is dedicated to Lou and Esta. As the 1989 *Tamakwa-Gram*, the camp newsletter, put it, "No one can fill the shoes of Lou, Esta, and Omer. But their spirit and traditions are perpetuated by a camp leadership that loved and learned from them. To this day, no young person leaves Tamakwa at summer's end without the feeling that he or she too knew, loved, and learned from Lou, Esta, and Omer."

At the end of every Friday service, Tamakwans sing their familiar song, followed by taps. And, as dusk closes in, they look out from the Slope over Tea Lake and finish with Unca Lou's benediction: "And now, may the Great Camper of all good campers be with us 'til we meet again."

Close behind Tamakwa's waters, Sloping hills of green,
Stands the fairest camp, For campers,
Fairest ever seen, Swell the chorus,
Let it echo, Over hill and vale,
Hail to thee , Our Camp Tamakwa,
Hail to thee, All hail.

. . .

Day is done, Gone the sun,
From the lakes, From the hills,
From the sky, All is well,
Safely rest, God is nigh.

. . .

And now, May the Great Camper,
Of all Good Campers,
Be with us 'til we meet again.

"Young folks, old folks, everybody come. Come to Tamakwa."

CANOE TRIPS

Trips come in past the girls' cabins, built in 1949 when the camp became co-ed. The current swim tower was built in 1992.

WENDIGO

On the same Cache Lake peninsula as Northway, but separated from the girls by a hemlock-and-pine-covered ridge, is Wendigo. Although this boys' camp grew out of Northway, it operates as a separate camp, with a different program and emphasis.

Wendigo was founded in 1965 largely because Northway was always searching for adequately trained canoe-trip guides. The name comes from a spirit represented by the wind in Algonquian legend. The camp was designed as a canoe-tripping outpost where boys could learn all of the campcraft and padding skills, and, at the same time, become familiar with Algonquin's canoe routes. The program has been a success. Many Wendigo graduates have since gone on to become Northway guides; of the eleven guides in 1993, only four were not former Wendigo campers.

Close examination of the cedar-strip canoe after returning from a ten-day canoe trip.

The camp has always been kept very small and it has a relaxed feel to it. Normally, there are no more than eight campers per session, and the peak enrolment for a summer has never exceeded thirty. The boys are usually between twelve and sixteen years old, and when they are in camp—which is only a couple of nights per session—they sleep in platform tents right at the water's edge.

Brookes Prewitt has been director at Wendigo since 1967. His on-site assistant director is Jim Spencer, also a former Northway guide. Jim says he used to feel a little anxious when new parents came to drop off their son. He wondered whether the small outpost was what the family expected, but he says now, "I don't apologize anymore. They picked Wendigo because of its size. That's what they want."

The main building looks more like a rustic cottage than a typical camp dining hall. The front wall is all windows, and a large deck

The main cabin is a pre-fabricated pine log building. In 1965, the last nail was driven just an hour before the first campers arrived.

faces Cache Lake and provides a view across to spectacular cliffs. Enjoying a rare afternoon in camp, the guys stretch out in deck chairs, work on carving projects, or play a game of cards. Inside, the Park map is spread out on the long table; the next route is being planned.

In camp, the boys sometimes make use of Northway's volleyball court, or they take a boat out for a sail, or maybe try a bit of archery. There's no schedule and each camper is free to pursue his own interests. One activity they share with Northway is canoe-building and paddle-making. The workshop is on the Wendigo side of the point, and there, each year, Jim works on a cedar and canvas canoe that will be added to the camp fleet at the end of the season.

Because Wendigo is so small, there's a real spirit of unity. No one is left out. Says Jim, "We don't foster any competitiveness. We focus on the individual person and development of their skills and personality."

From Wendigo, the boys head out on ten-day trips into the Park interior. The camp has sent groups to James Bay in the past, but the Park remains the most popular choice. Jim explains, "You get the variety, the wildlife, and you can still trip for days without seeing anyone."

The boys have a part in every aspect of trip planning. They help design the routes. Some are planned to cover long distances and familiarize them with more remote parts of the Park; others are more leisurely and allow for more instruction in the arts of map-reading or campcraft...or fishing. The boys also pack out their own trips, learning about food and equipment. Once they are off, the focus shifts to paddling skills, including practice in rapids. Northway guides lead the trips, and in that way the skills are passed on summer after summer.

The low-key feel of Wendigo is just the ticket for these campers. Most have mothers or sisters with a Northway connection. It's the canoe trips and Algonquin Park itself that have lured their families to this spot, and Jim Spencer can empathize. His family moved frequently when he was young, but the cottage on Cache Lake was his real home. Says Jim, "Algonquin had a tremendous impact on me. I always came back here, and this place was a real anchor." The Wendigo boys who return each summer and go on to become Northway guides feel the same way.

Jim Spencer builds the camps' canoes in Dwight and at camp.

Wendigo campers are on the peninsula they share with Northway a few nights per month. The boys sleep in platform tents in camp.

LIFE AT CAMP

GETTING THERE As the bus climbs gradually from Huntsville, so does the volume. The last illicit candy bars are shared out, the camp songs get louder, and kids scramble to collect their cards and comics. Then, at the end of a long avenue of maples, a familiar landmark appears—the Canadian flag flanked by the stone pillars of the west gate. For anyone who went to one of these camps after 1960, this view marked the homecoming to Algonquin Provincial Park.

Of course, the first campers didn't come by bus. Talk to any camper from earlier decades and the train trip to camp figures as an exciting memory in itself. The railway line through the south end of the Park was completed in 1896, and all of the campsites were originally chosen because of their proximity to this sole form of transportation. Gil Yager is one of many who recalls his trips to Pathfinder during the 1920s:

The old railway sign turned up at a cottage. A prank by a now-defunct rival camp?

Chief Norton had three or four Pullman cars. They left Rochester and stopped in Buffalo, and it was about a twenty-four-hour ride. It went up to Scotia Junction and we slept on the train overnight....We had breakfast around seven or eight o'clock the next morning at the hotel there. Then we took the train into Source.... At that time, there were four trains a day—two in each direction up and down the line here.

We'd get off at Source Lake Station and they threw all the trunks down the hill–they did make a chute finally. Then they caught and piled them all up on the dock. Everything went by a pontoon; they put three canoes together, lashed two-by-sixes across the top, and laid a deck. They could get ten or twenty people on that and then they hand-paddled them over to camp.

More than once, the strap across the bottom of the baggage chute broke; maverick trunks would float out into the lake. Motorboats made their appearance at Pathfinder in 1929, and after that,

Fred Lamke, the long-time maintenance man, started toting loads by barge. The old train station was moved to camp after the line closed in 1959, and now serves as The Candy Store for tuck sales. The original Source Lake Camp Pathfinder sign also found its way back to camp.

Wapomeo and Ahmek campers were let off at Taylor Statten Station at Sims Pits, the large sandy area north of Ahmek. Fran McColl was one of the female counsellors—nicknamed Inkie Mamas—at Ahmek during the late forties. They were in charge of the youngest cabin groups, the five-to-eight-year-old Incubators. Fran remembers waiting for her new charges on opening day. "It was a fairly long walk down through the forest. We sat out on the dining hall steps and waited for the first little kid to straggle in, dragging his paddle behind him." Wap campers then had to get over to the islands. Over the years, a succession of wooden launches, like the *Marmelwood*, were used for transport. When the train was discontinued, the girls got off buses at the Portage Store at the south

Most of the camps have to carry in luggage and supplies by boat.

end of Canoe Lake, and then paddled to the islands.

At Arowhon, a succession of large boats, each called *Lizzy,* helped ferry luggage and younger campers before the road was built into camp. Northway campers still paddle from the landing, as do returning Tanamakoon girls.

In early years, the Tanamakoon trunks were sent ahead, and the youngest campers arrived to find their beds made and a favourite stuffed toy propped up on the pillow. Tamakwa's campers still look forward to the last leg of their trip—the ride in the pointer boat from the landing. Rounding the bend on Tea Lake, a lone pine spreads out its familiar welcome, then camp swings into view.

The last moments of the approach to any camp are always charged with emotion. There's the anticipation—who will be in your tent or cabin—along with fears and sometimes more than a bit of homesickness. But a rush of warm hugs and handshakes engulfs the arrivals, and then they are swept off in a wave of boisterous enthusiasm.

FINDING YOUR WAY AROUND

The first thing to bombard the new arrivals is the list of places around camp. They're second nature to anyone who has been there before, but the newcomer needs a tour, guided by a seasoned interpreter.

To confuse matters, there's the peculiar slang veterans take for granted. At Northway, each girl stores her toiletries in an orange crate she drapes with fabric brought from home. But why are they called monuments? When you go to buy a toothbrush at most camps, look for the Tuck Shop, even though the only tuck you'll be lucky to find is chocolate bars or licorice whips. At the first meal, beware of breaking into applause, only to find that your camp is one of the four that says "How, How," instead. This habit dies hard; campers have been known to let "How, How" slip at

Tamakwa's Tuck Shop, with its shifting foundations on sand, was built in 1954.

movie theatres or even during toasts when camp sweethearts get married many years later. There are infirmaries or medicine lodges, and rest hours that can really be two hours long. And on the first day there are four hundreds. These are the obligatory swim tests of 400 metres. Voyageurs are the intermediate boys at Ahmek, the most honoured paddlers at Wendigo and Northway, and both the oldest boys and the best paddlers at Tamakwa.

When seeking the facilities, it's sometimes easier to follow your nose than to ask for directions. There's a confusing array of euphemisms: Biffies at Tamakwa, Forts at Pathfinder, Kybos at Ahmek, Flushies or Rosies at Wap, Hilltop and Peekaboo at Northway, in-cabin toilets at Arowhon, or the C.N. Tower and solar-powered Sun Life Building at Tanamakoon—two composters that sit on 10-foot-high foundations.

Predictably, the oldest campers are generally the farthest removed from main camp, and they all have their specific traditions. But confusingly, the Senior Cabin at Ahmek is now at the opposite end of camp from the Senior Section. After the cabin was built, the oldest boys were relocated to an area previously dubbed Matrimonial Row, for the married couples who lived there. Of more obvious origin is the name of the oldest tribe's home at Tanamakoon, Cree Flats, the patch of low ground beyond the swim docks. At Wapomeo, the senior girls have their separate Senior Island. They paddle to Main Island for all meals and some activities. The oldest sections on both islands also have their own special domain for gatherings: Shawnee Point on Main and Nahanni Rocks on Senior. Arowhon's Senior Girls have exclusive use of their Curve Dock, and at the opposite end of camp, there's The Point. If you cross the imaginary line at the birch tree without an invitation "you'll be liquidated," that is, tossed into the lake by the Senior Boys.

Lake names, too, have special significance. Veterans at Wendigo, tucked away from what little boat traffic there is on their lake, understand well the French root of Cache Lake. Each bay and inlet is truly hidden. When campers first came to Arowhon, the lake was called Buck, not Tepee. Knowing that makes sense of the title of the first play each summer, a satire entitled "Buck Lake." White's Lake was renamed after Mary Hamilton's camp in 1934, and Source Lake is at the headwaters of the Madawaska River.

Then there are other place names in the Park that evidence the camps' influence. Park authorities asked for suggestions for lake names from the childrens' camps in the early 1930s, when they used aerial photography to prepare maps for the first time. Nadine Lake was christened at Tanamakoon's request, in recognition of an outstanding camper and musician, Nadine Ysae. Wapomeo and Ahmek suggested the name for Tonakela Lake in 1931. The same year, Namakootchie's name was supplied by a Northway trip song of 1909 vintage, "We're the Namakootchies who camped on the Bonnechères." Pathfinder Lake, just west of Tom Thomson Lake, was also named in 1931.

After a few days at camp, the lay of the land becomes familiar to new campers, and campspeak is second nature. By the time parents arrive for their visit and tour, their son or daughter is throwing terms like "wash dips," "swim biscuit," "rosie leaves," and "shreck" around with the best of them.

A fire razed the first Ahmek dining hall and kitchen three days before campers arrived in 1937. The replacement was built the next year.

FINE DINING There's no denying that food is one of the most talked about subjects at camp. When the meals are good, camp is happy. Sometimes, the meals eaten *alfresco* are the most memorable. At Tanamakoon, every lunch is served buffet style outside the dining room—weather permitting. Most camps have some form of camp-wide cookout, too. Arowhon barbecues boneless chicken breast over charcoal on the kitchen's day off. Friday is special at Northway; it's hotdogs on the gas barbecue at the Point. Steaks on the grill welcome Wendigo boys in from trip, and on Thursdays, Wap and Ahmek cook all three meals over fires.

Tamakwa has a healthy afternoon-snack tradition. Lou Handler's brother-in-law was Mike Kraft, a Polish immigrant, and his familiar dialect is quoted to this day: "The keeds are good. Every afternoon, I feel they should have a leedle snack—fresh fruit. Everybody gets." After rest hour each day, the kids congregate in main camp for Tootsie Frootsie, as it has recently been named, and everybody still gets.

"And then I'd wish for a blazing campfire to welcome me as I'm returning home."

Trip food is also memorable, and even the disasters are polished off. Park authorities instituted a can and bottle ban in 1978, spurring a shift to dried and freeze-dried foods. Campers don't have to worry about tins jabbing them in the back anymore and the packs are lighter, but delicacies like condensed milk, canned bacon, and Tin Willy have disappeared. Some groups make bannock, a soda bread that is fried, baked over coals, or cooked in a reflector oven. Others still go in for the crusty loaves that hold their shape even after a week in the bread pack. S'mores, trip fudge, and tiger balls satisfy sugar cravings.

Back in camp, Northway campers started a baking program in 1993. They made pies, bread, and other treats using the wood stove in the library. The most popular recipe was a flourless cookie comprised solely of sugar and peanut butter.

For years, Wapomeo had one special lunch each month of rice and water called Meagre Meal. In the late 1920s, Wallace

Forgie, Tonakela's brother-in-law, established a camp for street kids outside Madras, India. The money saved on the meal at Wapomeo was sent each year in support of the Indian operation—Camp Tonakela.

Time spent in the dining hall is central to the camp experience. Those meals provide an interval when everyone comes together in happy confusion. Special memories include singsongs, skits, announcements, and—at Arowhon—the odd food fight. During the winter, Joanne Kates is a food critic. In a CBC radio interview she explained, "When they put chocolate éclairs down for dessert, I have to work hard to restrain myself...I love a good food fight." Campers flinging food is to be expected sometimes, she says, "But I think that if they're going to throw macaroni, it better have real cheddar cheese on it."

DAILY ROUTINE The word "routine" seems incongruous when you're talking about a place with dozens of kids between the ages of seven and sixteen, but there are regular everyday occurrences that are an integral part of the camp scene.

Every morning at Northway, the cook calls over to the first tent on the line: "Good Neighbour." From there, the wake-up call is passed along, with each group of girls shouting the name of the next tent. "Open Way, Airy Bluff, Sun Dew, Lone Pine, Hurricane Deck, Balsam Boughs, Deer Trail, Sunset Glow...Sunset Glow...Sunset Glow...." The call gets bogged down for a short time until particularly heavy sleepers are roused.

After breakfast at Ahmek and Wapomeo, there are the ubiquitous announcements, followed by a moment for reflection called Morning Meditation. At Wapomeo, staff and cabin groups take turns leading the program. It starts off with a poem, reading, or talk on the themes of nature, safety, or caring for others. Then campers put their heads down, and, putting aside thoughts about the slightly sticky table, take a few minutes to ponder loftier issues as they listen to a song or instrumental performance.

Tamakwa campers leave breakfast and assemble on the sandy plateau just in front of the dining hall facing the flagpole which stands in a grove of red pines. Since the group represents the United States and Canada equally, they sing both national anthems as the American and Canadian flags are raised.

Arowhon's daily activity auction. Joanne Kates sits beneath the stonework that dates back to the Camp of the Red Gods days.

A pause for cabin or tent clean-up comes next and many camps follow with inspection. As far back as the 1920s, inspection results were announced at dinner at Pathfinder. The boys jeered the worst, and the cleanest tent of the week earned candy bars. Today, the Ojibways at Tanamakoon vie for Algernon, a plush frog. His predecessor, Wilberforce the well-worn rabbit, hangs in the dining room. Under the Chief's directorship at Ahmek, parents were asked to describe on the application the skills they wished their sons to develop, and one mother cited tidiness. Her son won the eagle feather awards of the day for his neatness all summer, but he soon reverted to his old habits after his return home. Predictably, most camps have found it much more difficult to influence the housekeeping habits of the older campers.

While the kids are back in their sections at Arowhon, the activity instructors and section heads are meeting in the main lodge. Because Arowhon campers choose individualized programs for every period of the day, the spaces at activities have to be auctioned off. The section heads face each other across a table, and as instructors list the numbers they can accommodate each period, each section head yells out how many spots they want. It's frenzied and hectic, but it works.

Before they go to activities, Tanamakoon girls assemble in the lodge. There they learn a new song, listen to the announcements, and hear the day's program. At some point, Kim Smith announces important news from the outside world–like the Toronto Blue Jays' standings–then he tosses T-shirts and other lost articles to their owners, supplanting the usual Lost and Left collection box.

After lunch, comes another time-honoured rite: rest hour. Campers head back to their tents or cabins. It's a quiet time for reading, or writing letters, or–more rarely–for rest.

Mail is distributed in a different way at each camp. Northway campers line up at the bureau. Tanamakoon girls consult the daily mail

Northway campers head back to the tents for rest hour. This is "Sunset Glow."

list to see whether they should join a queue. Idelle Trellay has been in the Tamakwa office since 1973, and intercepting care packages from home has been part of her job for a number of those summers. She has even detected Tootsie Rolls stuffed into a Snoopy doll's arms, but the gum under the rim of a baseball hat got by her. At Wapomeo, the girls gather on the dock after dinner and sing the "Hymn of Thanksgiving" for flag lowering:

> *We praise thee our father,*
> *O hear our thanksgiving,*
> *For days rich with beauty,*
> *with joy and delight,*
> *For sunlight at noon-day,*
> *the blue tint of evening,*
> *The clear star at dusk,*
> *the quietness of night.*

Then, "Ding! Mail call!" they shout in one voice. The director has tapped a wind chime at closing, setting off the race to the sections for letters and packages.

ACTIVITIES The activities at camp can be divided between those that happen on, and in, water, and those that take place on land. Canoeing is such an integral part of the Algonquin camps that it deserves a separate look, but besides canoeing, there is a wide assortment of activities to suit every sort of camper.

Water Swimming and water safety are important at any camp—especially at camps situated on lakes, as these are. On arrival, every camper has to display basic competence, usually by swimming 400 metres, before they can participate in other waterfront recreation. Across the board, swimming is a compulsory activity; several camps offer instruction in Red Cross and Royal Life Saving Society levels.

Sailing is another activity that dates back to the early years. Northway and Tanamakoon held joint sailing regattas on Cache Lake, and Northway still has a small fleet of Optimist prams. At other camps, Ackroyds with sails of red, blue, and yellow stripes were popular in the early years. Albacores came later, but they have now largely been replaced by Lasers. Arowhon, with fifteen Snipes, has the second-largest fleet of this class in North America. Camp is still one of the first places a kid can learn to tie a bowline or feel the exhilarating tug on the tiller as a boat begins to heel.

Every other evening, some of the younger girls at Tanamakoon head for the docks with their "specials"—handmade fishing poles.

A newcomer on the waterfronts is boardsailing. Tamakwa, Arowhon, Wapomeo, and Ahmek have had thriving windsurfing programs since the early 1980s.

Also in recent years, kayaking programs have sprung up at Arowhon, Tamakwa, and Tanamakoon. A much older tradition is rowing at Pathfinder. Three of the cedar-plank boats date from the 1930s, and rowing was a regular activity between 1940 and 1980. Today, most of the rowboats stay pulled up on the shore, the silvered planking showing its age where the varnish has peeled away.

One informal waterfront pursuit is fishing. Every Thursday there's a fishing derby at the Ahmek canoe dock, and every second evening at Tanamakoon some of the younger girls gather at the waterfront with their "specials"—carefully selected branches wrapped with line. Only a few of these Ojibways appear squeamish about getting the worm on the hook; they're too absorbed in trying to snag Walter, the legendary trout who lives under the swim dock.

Camp Arowhon riders set out for the trails during the early 1950s.

Land Horseback riding was a feature at Tanamakoon and Tamakwa for a time, but today only Arowhon and the Taylor Statten camps have stables. At Arowhon there is one large riding ring, and campers can work toward awards: Thirds, Seconds, and Firsts. Also favoured by horse-lovers are the all-day trail rides with a cookout lunch.

Wapomeo and Ahmek share trails and a barn, although each has its own horses in separate wings of the barn. The rings are separate as well. Two events that involve the best equestrians from both camps, however, are the Hunt in July and the Three Day Event in August. The Hunt dates back to 1951. One exceptional rider acts the fox. The rest—the hounds and riders—pursue the fox over jumps and through the woods around Sims Pits. In 1953, Olympic equestrian John Rumble inaugurated the Three Day Event of dressage manoeuvres, a cross-country ride, and stadium jumping. Each year the names of the winning rider and his or her mount are added to the roster in Ahmek's dining hall.

Both Tamakwa and Pathfinder have added ropes courses in recent years. The aerial course at Pathfinder includes a catwalk 10 metres off the ground, and a bold leap to a trapeze from the top of the 8-metre Pamper Pole. The course is great for developing co-operative skills. Last summer, when Nate started across the Heebie Jeebies at Pathfinder, all of the other boys dropped what they were doing to call out encouragement. A nervous camper below was getting a few quiet words from his tent mate, "It's your choice, Andy. No one is going to make you do anything. We all know how you feel." There's a climbing program at Pathfinder, too. Once the boys have learned the basics on the practice wall at camp, they're off on field trips to places like Ragged Falls.

Some of the Algonquin camps have had to be resourceful to offer tennis. Arowhon, with its level site, had no trouble situating four courts. Ahmek and Wapomeo were able to add courts in 1953 when the low area west of main camp

Mastering the catwalk at Pathfinder.

10 metres up on the Adventure Course.

was filled in. It was Tay Statten who wanted to introduce tennis, because it was a sport that campers could take back to the city and enjoy there. Tamakwa gave up its full-sized courts on the low ground by the swim docks because of heaving caused by frost. Their solution is half-court tennis on an artificial surface up behind the dining hall. Tanamakoon's court has a loose surface for the same reason. In 1935-36, Pathfinder "power crews" hauled clay by pontoon across from the railway landing to build the lone clay court. Without more use, the ferns and moss will gradually reclaim it for the forest.

Each of the camps has an arts and crafts program. A few include pottery. Paddle-making is popular at Wendigo, Northway, and Tanamakoon. Photography has been in demand at intervals; Northway's darkroom, in a cubbyhole under the dining hall, produced camp postcards for a time. Wapomeo's unique weaving program has waxed and waned over the years. In his biography of Taylor Statten, C. A. M. Edwards recounts:

Much of his [the Chief's] spending was impulsive and many of his purchases, once they reached camp, rapidly fell into disuse. He got the idea that if the girls at Camp Wapomeo were going to do weaving as a camp activity they should have a thorough understanding of the hobby. He therefore bought spinning wheels, carding equipment, a huge old-fashioned loom (1822 vintage), and weaving equipment of all sorts and he even contemplated importing sheep into Algonquin Park to provide the wool.

Recently, the program has been resurrected. The Weavery sign, with its accompanying shuttle, has been moved from the arts and crafts building to where it now swings, outside the new weavery, a former camper cabin.

Tamakwa has the only in-camp radio station. The equipment was salvaged by David Stringer from York University, and CAMP RADIO 1100 broadcasts over a small radius a couple of hours a day. Campers run the program, writing their own scripts and selecting music.

The nature and campcraft activities take full advantage of the woods environment. The woodcraft program is one of the most popular of all activities at Tanamakoon. A camp motto defines it as "the art of finding one's way in the wilderness and getting along well by utilizing Nature's

storehouse." The campers learn to use a compass, build one-match fires, wield an axe, and perform first aid, among other practical skills. At Ahmek, renowned naturalists Jack Miner and Stuart Thomson instructed in the early days, and one of camp was named for ranger Mark Robinson, who shared his immense knowledge of the Park at camp. In 1979, campers and staff built a nature trail, another successful addition to Ahmek's ecology program.

The popularity of archery has fluctuated over the years. At some camps, the site was moved every few years as more popular activities needed space, but at Tanamakoon archery has maintained fairly consistent interest. Campers there work on awards; the levels are colour-coded to the rings of the bull's-eye from white up to gold.

Team sports and other athletic pursuits have greater or lesser importance depending on the space available. Pathfinder has a somewhat lumpy baseball field where the senior staff, Nine Old Men, take on the campers. Northway's volleyball court is tucked away among the trees up on the ridge. Wapomeo girls paddle over to make use of Ahmek's baseball diamond or new basketball court close by. At Tamakwa, quoits, basketball, volleyball, and other land sports are programmed into the day. Mountain bikes are a recent addition at Tanamakoon. Unscheduled tetherball games fill gaps between activities at a number of camps; Tanamakoon girls swing on the large tire beside the dining room in their spare moments.

Drama activities hold a special place at camps. Whether in weekly show nights, skits to announce special events, or major musical productions at the end of the month, every kid has the opportunity to go on stage. Chicken wire, papier-mâché, huge sheets of brown paper, and tempera are hurriedly transformed into Oz or a 1950s soda shop. Bathrobes, castoffs, and a bit of make-up produce mikados or southern belles. Improvisation and making do are key. Stars rehearse lines on canoe trip, and leading actors and actresses sometimes give up most other activities to work on the production in the final days before the show.

Northway campers have an added challenge. Since trips go out at different times, the whole cast is never in camp together until the day before

the big play. Campers practise their lines in small groups, and the blocking is worked out at the last minute. The campers send out invitations to the cottagers, many of whom are Northway alumni, and this audience assembles on play night in front of the lodge. The open-front log building has been the home of Northway's theatre since campers built it in 1917.

Ahmek's Log Cabin Theatre was built in 1927 at the head of Wigwam Bay. Drama productions flourished under the direction of top-notch, enthusiastic drama instructors. Unfortunately, the theatre was destroyed in 1957, when Hurricane Audrey raged through and the creek rose so much that the foundations were swept into the bay. Productions moved into the dining hall following this loss, but the drama program never regained its previous momentum.

During the early 1930s, Dora Mavor Moore was drama instructor at Tanamakoon. She designed the theatre, and campers helped with construction. The stage is at the bottom of a slight slope and it is open at

Arowhon's main lodge holds dozens of plaques. This one depicts 1993's shows.

Northway's open-front lodge, built by campers in 1917.

Tanamakoon's theatre was built in the early 1930s. Dora Mavor Moore, the drama instructor at the time, designed it.

the front, where a gracefully curved log forms the proscenium. There are performances throughout the summer, but the most involved show is a serious dramatic production at the end of August. In 1993, the campers performed  "Colours in the Storm," about Tom Thomson; playwright Jim Betts personally tailored his script to make it more appropriate for the camp audience. Interestingly, Dora Mavor Moore's granddaughter had a key role. The highlight of the season for the girls was taking the show on the road to a well-attended public performance at the Park's Pog Lake Outdoor Theatre.

Arowhon's theatre program was launched by Lorne Greene. He was a drama student at Queen's University when Lillian Kates lured him to camp with promises of running his own theatre. Once he arrived, he tried repeatedly to get her to point out the lounge—the term for cabaret-style stages of the day. When he finally stopped her in the dining hall and asked with exasperation, "Where is my theatre?" she responded, "You're standing in it." To which reply, the young actor mused, "Well, it's a very rustic lounge." Every summer, the girls stage an original revue called "Rustic Lounge" at the beginning of July. Lorne Greene did eventually get a theatre. Built according to his design, the rec hall seats three hundred.

Tamakwans also have a love of the stage. In fact, some have gone on to entertainment careers, like former campers Gilda Radner and Chevy Chase, and filmmakers Sam Raimi and Mike Binder. Tamakwa even came to the big screen in 1993 with Binder's film, *Indian Summer*. The camp was transformed into a movie set in September 1992, with some present-day campers coming back to play as extras. A number of log structures, including the swim tower and a new archway, were built and instantly aged, and they look as if they've been at Tamakwa forever. Unfortunately, the fall colour hadn't co-operated when filming started, so in true camp spirit, the director made do; portable trees complete with silk autumn foliage stood in.

CANOEING At the heart of the Algonquin camps' programs is the canoe. It represents transportation, freedom, and more. A canoe heeled over on its side, slipping soundlessly across the reflection of puffy clouds, is a picture of complete harmony. All is fluid. New campers, of course, have to learn basic safety and bow strokes before they head out, but competent solo paddling is the ultimate objective. With this exposure grows a deep respect for the canoe itself.

All of the camps in Algonquin have fleets of cedar canvas-covered canoes. The venerable oldtimers are Chestnuts and Peterboroughs, but

A canoe heeled over on its side, slipping soundlessly across the reflections of clouds is the picture of perfect harmony. Preparing for the Voyageur test at Tamakwa.

there are newer boats, too. Many were built by former campers who have taken a love of canoes that was sparked at camp and made it their full-time passion. Jack Hurley, Pathfinder alumnus, shares a workshop in Dwight with Jim Spencer of Northway-Wendigo. Dan Gibson Jr., who grew up on Canoe Lake, has had a hand in many of Tamakwa's newer canoes. Tanamakoon's canoes come from Hugh Stewart.

Three of the most recent additions to the Pathfinder fleet were donated in memory of members of the Pathfinder family. Special plaques are attached to the bow decks. When the canoe dedicated to long-time waterfront staff Norm Roggow arrived in 1993, the excitement rippled through the camp. Each boy who spotted the new arrival came over to take a closer look. "Hey Mac," said one, "Is that a new canoe? Awesome!" Although some camps have added aluminum or plastic canoes for tripping, the wooden boats are the ones that seasoned paddlers continue to choose for quiet sunrise paddles.

A skilled singler at Ahmek practises pivots for his upcoming Master Canoeist test.

Wapomeo is also home to two 42-foot war canoes that were custom-built by the Peterborough Canoe Company in 1925. They are the only canoes of their kind, and still used regularly today. Senior campers paddle them to get to every meal and for trips across the lake.

One of the builders involved with construction of the war canoes was Stan Murdoch. When Ahmek was searching for someone to repair canoes, the Peterborough company referred them to Stan. He arrived in 1926, saw the war canoes there, and stayed until his retirement in 1975. The Ahmek shop continues to be a year-round operation; two hundred canoes require continual upkeep. Bill Statten looked after canoe maintenance for a number of years, and Dave Standfield has recently taken over the enormous task. Stan's recipe for canvas filler remains a closely guarded secret of the Ahmek canoe shop.

The paddling styles at many of these camps have common roots. Ahmek and Wapomeo trace their canoeing traditions back to Bill Stoqua of Golden Lake. Omer Stringer had an immeasurable influence on the

Algonquin camps and others, too. His booklet, *The Canoeist's Manual*, helped define national standards. The biography in that publication describes him: "He is a lazy perfectionist who believes in controlling his canoe with precision and minimum effort." Omer took his entertaining demonstrations to many camps, but naturally, Tamakwa enjoyed a very close relationship with him. In fact, Omer built many of the newer canoes at Tamakwa before his death in 1988.

Another element that several of the camps share is the canoeing standards program that was set by the Ontario Camping Association in the 1930s. The Beginner through to Master Canoeist awards are still in use at Ahmek, Wapomeo, and Tanamakoon.

Each of the camps celebrates its best paddlers. At Tamakwa, the highest level is the Voyageur. Candidates are judged by a panel of all of the other Voyageur canoeists in camp. Patterns, landings, teaching, windy weather paddling, and canoe care are some of the areas in which aspiring Voyageurs must demonstrate absolute control and finesse. Master canoeists at Wapomeo and Ahmek are

Omer's demonstrations were famous.

The headstand made a grand finale.

also put through the paces, and they have to perform all manoeuvres equally well on their "bad" side. Special keelless canoes are reserved for the exclusive use of these Master paddlers. At Arowhon, First Class canoeists are honoured on a special plaque.

Whether it's a purple V or a small maple leaf, the symbols that mark the highest canoeing achievements at camp are held in great regard.

CANOE TRIPS While other camps truck groups to the Park for special trips, the Algonquin camps enjoy the privilege of having Ontario's oldest and most famous park right in their backyard. Naturally, canoe-tripping is a central part of the camp experience for these girls and boys. As Fanny Case wrote in her account, "The Story of Northway Lodge," in 1942:

Canoe trips are the crowning experience of camping in this country. There is a tang in the deep and lasting memories of camp that undoubtedly is derived largely from this mettle-testing experience.

Camp directors in Algonquin Park and similar country know that this is true.

Canoe trips are full of both physical and psychological challenges. The first day out, untrained arms ache a bit, and packs are heavy. Arriving at a portage, campers learn to help each other steady and unload the canoe. The insurmountable hill is conquered, the "turtled" camper hauled to her feet, the first canoe carry applauded. Campers learn to work together to put up the tent or to gather wood so they can cook supper. Couchie of Wapomeo describes the net result:

> *The canoe trip really created a bond within the group.... Teamwork was the key to a successful trip and co-operation was necessary when you were living so closely for twenty-four hours a day, for two weeks or longer. I think it's an experience you can't get anywhere else.*

The sense of achievement is both immediate and long-lasting. Campers learn that they can accomplish things they never thought they could. They learn teamwork, but also self-reliance; they learn that they are able to rise to the occasion and take initiative themselves. These feelings resurface in their later lives when other challenges arise.

Repeatedly, campers cite canoe trip as the best experience of the summer. Some catch a glimpse of a moose, water plants dripping from its muzzle. A few are treated to a rare chorus of wolf howls, an enduring symbol of Algonquin's wild spirit. All experience nights when brilliant stars reflecting from the lake's still surface burn twice as brightly, or days when a cool, grey mist dampens everything but spirit. As Marguerite, who comes all the way from Paris, France, each summer says, "My friends say I'm lucky to have camp in Canada. When we are going on canoe trip, we can paddle for five days and never see roads and buildings.... Algonquin Park is beautiful."

Not surprisingly, there are many canoe-trip rituals. At Northway, the counsellor walks around the dining hall at breakfast, places her hands on a girl's shoulders and invites her out on a trip that will leave that day. Miss Case thought that keeping the trips secret until the last moment would avoid pre-trip jitters. After Morning Council, the rest of the camp gathers at the docks to see off the trip with a chorus of "Au Large trippers, Au Large trippers, Au Large trippers; You're going to leave us now." Northway can trace many of its tripping practices to Ernest Finlayson, who, as a University of Toronto graduate in forestry, set guidelines for the earliest trips. An Algonquin Park guide, Charlie

"Tripping—that is the life for me, Algonquin Park is where I long to be. With my pals, packs, and paddles, And my Ahmek canoe...."

Skuce, followed; he was head guide at Northway for thirty-four years. Wendigo places such an emphasis on canoe trips, that even the time at base camp is spent in preparation. During a three-and-a-half-week session, campers go out on two ten-day trips which leaves only three or four nights in camp.

Longer trips outside Algonquin have become as popular at Wapomeo as they are at Ahmek. During the late 1960s, there was great concern that the camps would have to leave Algonquin when their leases expired. The Taylor Statten camps started investigating other areas, and, as a result, they acquired an outpost in Temagami in 1969. The first Quetico Park trip was in 1965. As part of a centennial year cross-country canoe relay, Ahmek and Wap were to complete the Boundary Waters leg. The 1965 exploratory trip charted the route, and Quetico has been a mainstay of the long-trip program ever since. Trips up to fifty days long to LaVérendrye, Kipawa, Killarney, and Biscotasing have also been added.

Canoe packs drying at summer's end.

Pathfinder's Dud-Larry Trading Post.

Tanamakoon recently acquired a 24-foot Voyageur canoe and the camp now sends out one special war-canoe trip each summer. The first trip in 1992 was along the French River; Georgian Bay was the destination the following summer.

Pathfinder has had two longer James Bay trips in recent years. The destination was a surprise both years. The night before the Mattagami River trip departed in 1993, staff misled campers with speeches about the wonderful Temagami area. When the news broke about the true destination, the stamping and shouting carried on for some time. But more characteristic of Pathfinder's tripping program are the Algonquin trips. One father was so pleased with the effect of those trips on his two boys that he contributed funds for a tripping building in the early 1940s. It is called the Dud-Larry Trading Post after those brothers. In the back room of Dud-Larry hangs a Park map with all the routes Pathfinder trips have covered during the summer traced in marker; the map is a dense web of thick black lines.

When former Tanamakoon girls think of trips, many remember the native guides of the old days. Matt Lavally used to whittle in the evenings on the trips he guided, and he often presented small carved treasures to campers: a little paddle, or canoe, or a spreading fan made from a single piece of wood. The girls never knew that he carried with him a bag of these ready-made gifts, carved the previous winter. Matt led Ojibway trips until the year he died, at eighty-four years of age. Matt's brother Henry was another favourite because of his sense of humour. He sent one eager camper rushing along the Happy Isle portage in search of a Coca-Cola machine.

Welcoming trips back is another custom at several camps. The call goes down the tent line at Northway when someone spots returning trips. The girls form a kick line on the swim docks as they sing their welcome song. When Tanamakoon trippers return, the rest of camp greets them with the song "Welcome Trippers, Hale and Strong." That evening, the new arrivals wear white shirts in the dining room, and each group sings the song they composed while they were away. This is such

Northway campers gather at the docks to form a kick line when trips return.

a tradition that the Tanamakoon Songbook is filled with trip songs that have stuck. Tamakwans gather at their trip docks to greet returning trips when the bell rings after rest hour. Tootsie Frootsie and "We welcome you" greet the incoming canoes. It used to be a tradition at Pathfinder that each group dress up or present a skit on the way in. According to camp legend, one group paddled in with green and grey canoes. In order to get closer to the skinny-dipping girls on Canoe Lake, the Pathfinder campers had painted over their red canoes with Wapomeo colours on their rest day at Burnt Island Lake!

Not every camper takes to trip, but Couchie tells a Wapomeo story with a familiar ending. One camper was very reluctant to go on a canoe trip and she complained even to the director. The day her cabin returned, Couchie says, "Her mom and dad were in camp waiting anxiously...and I was too. She paddled in, threw her arms around her parents, and then she saw me. 'Thank you,' she said, 'for making me go on that trip. I had a wonderful time.'"

13 Day

Paddling away from the shores of safety

From the shores of knowing and expectation

Not knowing what to expect

How to feel

Scared and unsure

Insecure

Not knowing

If the freedom will live up to

The standards of what it is made out to be

Discovery and surprise

Seek with open eyes

Change

Life

Learning to survive

And to revive

When one's energy is lost

And the motivation dies down

But to round that Bend again

One appreciates

One realizes

What they have just experienced

The feeling of safety

Returns

But one longs for the wilderness

The freedom, and discovery

Of their home away from home

> Jodi Kovitz, Tamakwa camper
> Cabin 49er 6–Senior Girls' contribution for the
> Centennial of Algonquin

TAKING CARE Care of the campers, the camp, and the Park are always priorities at the Algonquin camps.

On the waterfront, the camps use the buddy system and peg or tag boards. Each camp has additional water safety procedures. The swim search siren at Wapomeo jolts everyone into action; the island and the pools are thoroughly searched if a camper or staff forgets to tag out. An extra safeguard at Tamakwa is the Eye-Full Tower. From the lookout, the person on duty can alert other staff if a sailboat has dumped or a windsurfer is having trouble.

"Buddies!" Dousing a lifeguard during Ahmek's General Swim.

Drills keep safety skills honed. The swim search siren jolts everyone into action at Wapomeo.

Before they go out in boats, campers have to know what to do if they tip. They practise putting on a Personal Flotation Device in water and they study basic safety rules. More than one boater can attribute surviving a serious situation in later life to rules learned at camp.

Fire is another worry. Most of these camps are water-access only. Staff have to be trained to respond quickly to an emergency themselves. Some practise bucket brigades and evacuation procedures. Others train a special fire crew to run pumps.

The camp facilities themselves also require care. A group of Pathfinder staffmen shows up early each spring to help with major repairs or construction jobs. Most of the other camps have a maintenance staff that works behind the scenes, making sure the physical plant is in good shape. Some work year-round repairing roofs, building new cabins, or shoring up foundations. Boats and motors also require constant repair. For the most part, when the campers leave in the fall, the buildings stand empty to suffer the ravages of a harsh winter.

The Shop-built 1936—where repairs to Wap and Ahmek's 200 wood canoes are done.

The maintenance crews hold at bay the unceasing influence of Algonquin's climate, and the names of a few who made significant contributions are still familiar to present campers. There was Pathfinder's Fred Lamke who, equipped with an axe, could do just about anything. He worked for thirty years at the camp, until the early seventies, and he spent many winters bringing in the ice; his horse was stabled underneath the present-day workshop. Ahmek handyman Archie Hutton is immortalized in the show night song: "It's Show Night, It's Show Night. The curtain's up in an hour. The Waps are a-comin', the whole camp is hummin', and Archie is turning on power." Tanamakoon remembers George May. Muriel Hall, who first came to the camp in 1941, and is still helping out with the kitchen and housekeeping, remembers George's hand in construction, his magic with troublesome pumps, his winters of cutting ice, and more than a few good stories. One day when George's wife, Willa, and Muriel were in the kitchen, they heard scratching at the door.

Thinking it was George with a load of wood, Willa opened the door to greet a large black bear.

Those who use the Park also have a duty to care for it. Several camps have participated in clean-up and portage maintenance programs over the years. During World War II, the camps' role was especially important. With Park staff at a minimum, campers were formally deputized as Algonquin Park Auxiliary Rangers in 1941. Each camp assumed responsibility for maintaining portages, keeping campsites in order, and for fire ranging in a particular assigned area.

Dan Strickland, Chief Park Naturalist, addressed representatives from the camps in August of 1993. He remarked that, apart from the people who work in Algonquin, the childrens' camps have been in the Park the longest of any group and they have made the most extensive use of it. With that history comes an obvious love of the Park and the collective responsibility to treat it well.

PRACTICAL JOKES Tamakwa is a fun-loving family. The shrecks—good-natured practical jokes—are legendary. Three of last summer's Pioneers, intermediate-age girls, explained the ground rules: "You can't mess up anybody's stuff and you can't be mean." When their cabin got back from

canoe trip, all of the lightbulbs were missing from their section. The girls found them—the next morning—strung from the roof of the dining hall. In the late 1950s, the campers arrived at breakfast one morning to find that all the cutlery had disappeared. It was only discovered when it was time to play the national anthems for flag-raising; forks, knives, and spoons were stuffed into the upright piano, inside pillowcases. Linda Saltzman recounted another shreck in a 1960s edition of "Beaver Cuttings," the annual camper publication: "One very, very hot day the entire camp was called into main camp after Rest Hour 'to get salt tablets.' But instead of salt tablets, we all got soaked—and shocked—by water being sprayed from the fire hoses positioned on top of the mess hall."

Practical jokes didn't always get a favourable reception. Charles Geyer remembers running a Pathfinder counsellor's sleeping bag up the flagpole. When Chief Norton called the boys to his office, "you knew you'd done something wrong. He would say, in his famous words, he was 'chagrined' and he'd make you feel pretty guilty." The most "chagrining" pranks drew several days of peeling potatoes.

Of course, old campers won't tell their best practical jokes on record, especially for inclusion in a book. We'll have to leave them to word of mouth.

Archery's popularity has fluctuated over the years, but safety and proper care of equipment have always been part of the program.

Each of the Algonquin camps has medical staff in residence.

Canoes are carefully stored for winter. Three of the newer canoes were donated in memory of members of the Pathfinder family.

A Sunday morning at Tanamakoon.

MOMENTS OF REFLECTION Spend any time in the Park and you will begin to sense that you are part of something much bigger than the physical here and now. For some, this involves a sense of history. For others, an affirmation of a Creator. And for all, an awe of nature's enduring beauty and power. Young people at all the camps take time out from the regular activities for some quiet introspection about larger issues of a spiritual nature.

Every Sunday, campers and staff file into the open-air chapel at Tanamakoon to subdued song. Before the 1930s, chapel was held in the lodge, but the campers felt the services might inspire greater reverence if they were held under the trees. The girls picked the spot overlooking the lake: it is ringed with a cedar railing they built. A canopy of pines arches over the contemplative assembly, and the thoughts expressed there each week reaffirm Grey Owl's words: "There is a sanctity in the forests of great trees, like that of old cathedrals."

The first Sunday services at Wapomeo were held with Ahmek on the point of land that later became Chubby's Island. When the seniors moved to Big Wapomeo, the older girls invited the rest of camp to their island, and a field organ was carried down to Shawnee Point at the south end. The whole group, wearing white, sat on the rocks and looked out over Canoe Lake as they sang. Today, chapel is held on the lodge steps, and many campers still wear white. The girls themselves take turns picking a theme and leading a non-denominational service.

Since 1940, Pathfinder boys have gathered for their services at the Jean Norton Chapel. The chapel was built by a staffman that year as a memorial to Chief Norton's daughter who died as a teenager. The site, at the end of its own trail, exudes peace. Rows of logs form semicircular seating up a low incline and cedars create a fragrant bower. On Sunday afternoons, the boys congregate and a senior staffman leads a non-denominational talk.

Ahmek sings a grace before every meal. The lyrics for each of the three graces were written during the 1930s by the Chief's friend, theologian Dr. Eustace Haydon. Murray Adaskin composed the music for the "Evening Grace," and both it and Michael Head's "Morning Grace" were published by the English firm Bosey and Hawkes. Although high-spirited boys have had their fun with the emphasis from time to time, the stirring message of the grace has struck a chord with three generations, both at Ahmek and Wapomeo:

Evening Grace

Let us give thanks that life is high adventure,

That unscaled heights await us, await us everyday.

Let us be glad for work and love and laughter,

For loyal friends and comrades,

and comrades on the way.

The evening shadows, gather

round the sunset.

This day will join our long lost

yesterdays.

As builders of the better world we seek,

May we be wise to use each

newborn day,

Let us give thanks.

Fanny Case wrote, "The majesty of the trees is inspiring...." At Northway, "The open book of nature was before us in all of its glory, to be met firsthand. How to open our eyes and ears is our quest." One place where Northway and Wendigo campers seek this is La Lumière. A path cushioned with hemlock cones and needles

winds its way into the forest to a place that has always been a spot for quiet contemplation. Crumbled cedar walls and a roof made of scooped logs are all that remain of the first Lumière; bunchberry, wintergreen, and moss are slowly engulfing it. In its place stands a new cedar structure of warm, copper-hued beams. Dedicated to the memory of a former guide, the new Lumière continues to be a place where campers and staff go to listen to the white-throats and open their senses to the peace and glory of nature.

Friday evening observances at Arowhon include lighting candles and a blessing at dinner. The tone during dinner is subdued, and the meal is followed by a contemplative talk. At other times, when Arowhon campers seek some quiet "timeout," they too have special places. A few minutes' walk along a trail is Hidden Lake; the view from the lookout takes in a small pond and marsh where tall grasses whisper, lilypads sparkle, and the occasional moose wanders by. It's a good spot to go alone to

"The majesty of the trees is inspiring." Northway's first Lumière was built in 1910.

think about things or to take aside a child who needs some quiet time for serious discussion.

Drawing on the same Jewish traditions as Arowhon, Tamakwa also has observances on Friday nights. The campers run a non-religious service on the Slope. Sometimes the talks focus on why camp and Algonquin Park are so special. Campers repeatedly affirm that they learn to appreciate nature here in a way that they wouldn't elsewhere, and they carry that back to the city with them at the end of every summer. Idelle Trellay says it well: "There's no other place in the world like it. You can reach out and touch the stars, and you will never find rainbows like they are here." Tamakwan Jim Lavine points out the enduring influence of experiences in the Park:

> I think if you take a survey, you'll find many of the early campers are people who are responsible today and are carrying out in their community lives the lessons they learned.... Much of that comes from the start here in the natural setting of the Park and the training they get at camps.

At the close of every day, campers at Tanamakoon, Tamakwa, and Pathfinder take part in a time-honoured rite, Taps. Sometimes they are played on a trumpet or battered horn, or the campers will join hands as they sing:

> Day is done
> Gone the sun
> From the lakes,
> From the hills,
> From the sky,
> All is well
> Safely rest
> God is nigh.

THINGS THAT GO BUMP IN THE NIGHT What better place to get pleasantly scared out of your wits than around a dying fire with your camp friends? Lots of legends and ghost stories are brought to camp, but a few seem to be truly indigenous. Some have spread to more than one camp: Jacque the Mad Axeman has appeared at both Tamakwa and Arowhon, Northway girls claim Pathfinder's George Liederhaus as their own, and a baby-blue canoe seems to be a common conveyance for crazed villains in the Park. We can only imagine how this dissemination occurred, but two of the best tales are repeated here.

George Liederhaus and the Baby-Blue Canoe *(as related by Mac Rand and Alex Thomson)* George was the son of an early Park ranger. He was a large boy, and, equipped with a baby-blue canoe made by his father, he became a ranger himself at the young age of fifteen. In time, George married, and he brought his wife and young son to live with him during the summers on White Trout Lake. Those readers familiar with the Park probably know of this cabin and the fire tower George manned on what is now Big Trout.

One day, as George paddled in from patrol, he saw smoke rising from his post. He arrived to find his cabin burned to the ground; his wife and son had perished. After this tragedy, George became a recluse, and he gradually grew wilder and wilder. There were infrequent sightings. Sometimes at dusk, a tripper would spot a lone paddler with a double-headed axe in the bow of his canoe. Years later, when a friend of George's father dumped in rapids, the old ranger regained consciousness, wrapped warmly in blankets. He caught just a glimpse of a mysterious hulk lumbering off into the forest.

Several years later, a group of city folk were having a wild party on a campsite in the Park. They were drinking heavily, not paying attention to the cries of their children in the tents. George went berserk at this neglect, and with his axe, he took the lives of all but one of the adults. The last survivor died relating the bloody events to police in hospital. Authorities scoured the bush, searching for the madman. One search party finally caught him in a net, and he was taken to jail.

One night, not much later, the guards were drunk. A cigarette flicked carelessly into a wastepaper basket turned the jail into an inferno. As the negligent keepers fled, roars came from the cell, and the crazed prisoner bent the molten bars and made good his escape.

One person who has actually spotted George Liederhaus is Jack Hurley. He often returns to Pathfinder to tell the boys about George and about his own close calls. When he was a young boy, out fishing at sunset with his trip's headman on Grassy Bay, the headman knocked Jack swiftly to the bottom of the canoe with his paddle to avoid George's detection.

All campers who trip in the Park should keep on the watch for blue paint on rocks at the start of a portage. They provide warning that George is just ahead. It's prudent to change the route or, at the very least, hold back for a few hours.

The Tom Thomson Mystery As true as the George Liederhaus story must be, the mysterious events surrounding Tom Thomson's death at Canoe Lake have drawn more widely published attention.

Tom Thomson first came to Algonquin in 1912. He was becoming an artist of some note, and he painted Algonquin's haunting landscape in all its rugged beauty. From 1914 to 1917, Thomson made Canoe Lake his base for painting in the spring. He guided or ranged in the summer, went on sketching trips again in the fall, and then returned to Toronto to paint his full-sized canvases during the winter. Like no one else, Thomson was able to capture the brilliant spirit of the Park's untamed wilds, and he painted several of his most significant works, such as *Jack Pine* and *A Northern Lake,* in Algonquin.

Tom's friend Shannon Fraser owned Mowat Lodge on the west shore of Canoe Lake. Fraser reported last seeing the artist setting out from Mowat on July 8, 1917. A week later, Thomson's body was found floating off Kiowa Rocks at Big Wapomeo Island. The body was badly decomposed, so there was a hasty autopsy. Death was attributed to drowning, even though there was no water in the lungs. Chief Ranger Mark Robinson saw the corpse; he noted a bruise on the left

temple and fishing line wrapped sixteen or seventeen times around the victim's ankle. Thomson's body was hurriedly interred at the little grave site behind Mowat.

Two nights later, an undertaker arrived with instructions to exhume the coffin and transfer it to the Thomson family plot in Leith, near Owen Sound. Shannon Fraser took the undertaker up to the grave site, and left him there alone to do his work. Shannon always maintained that the casket he subsequently helped load onto the train was not heavy enough to hold a body.

In 1956, several Ahmek staff were at Canoe Lake for Thanksgiving weekend. Jack Eastaugh, Judge William Little, Leonard "Gibby" Gibson, and Frank Braucht ventured up to the Mowat plot one wet evening, and started to dig. As the crowd was sitting down to Thanksgiving dinner at Ahmek, Jack walked in with a tibia and asked Dr. Harry Ebbs how big he thought the man who belonged to that bone might have been. Harry held it up against his calf and replied, "Oh, about my size." They contacted authorities to let them know about the discovery.

The following weekend an official party, including the original four men, were back to dig up the mysterious remains. An Ontario Provincial Police officer was present; when a shovel struck wood, he reached down and pulled up a small metal plaque. "My God," he pretended to read, "Tom Thomson." Unfortunately the mystery was not solved that easily; the nameplate was blank. Forensic studies in Toronto identified the remains as belonging to a native, but Jack Eastaugh maintains, "I can't put anyone else in that grave—and certainly not an Indian."

So the mystery of who was in that grave has not been settled to everyone's satisfaction. The cause of death is also an area of great speculation. Daphne Crombie, a close friend of Shannon's wife, Annie Fraser, was interviewed by Ronald Pittaway in Toronto in January 1977. She related what Mrs. Fraser had told her about Tom's last night.

> *Tom and George and another guy had a party. They were all pretty good drinkers.... Tom asked Shannon Fraser for the money that he owed him because he had to go and get a new suit.... Anyway, they had a fight and Shannon hit Tom, knocked him down by the fire grate, and Tom had a mark on his forehead. I don't know where it was. Annie told me all this.... Of course, Fraser was terrified.... My conception is that he took Tom's body and put it into a canoe and dropped it in the lake.*

Is it possible that Fraser tied a rock around the artist's leg to postpone discovery of the body? Another account says that Tom was prone to mild seizures. Could he have had an attack while fishing near shore, stumbled and hit his head?

Mary Northway, a Smoke Lake cottager, once wrote about an eerie encounter in an unpublished booklet entitled "Nominigan: A Casual History." She was not the only person to have the type of experience she described in "The Phantom Canoe (Tom Thomson)," dated October 1933:

> *...the voice of my guide shattered the silence; "They're coming out to meet us from the portage." And I, turning toward the sunset, saw a man kneeling in a canoe that slowly came toward us.*
>
> *"So they are," I answered, "I guess we are pretty late." My guide turned from his course in order that we might better meet our herald, now a little less than a hundred yards away. I raised my voice and called and waved my hand, while my guide kept paddling toward the camper. But there was no response for, even as we looked, the canoe and its paddler, without warning or sound, vanished into nothingness, and on the undisturbed lake were only our lonely selves and the shrieking of a loon.*

Page Statten was with the group the day the corpse was exhumed from the Mowat grave site in 1956. As he so correctly puts it, "The mystery goes on and we're glad it does."

Statten's campers erected a totem at the Thomson cairn in 1930.

A sunset paddle on Canoe Lake.

GREAT HONOURS Each of the camps has its own roster of great achievements and most honoured skills. Some honours are earned by contest and others are conferred on campers in recognition of other contributions to camp life.

The Ahmek Waterman's Award A triangular plaque in the Ahmek dining hall represents the threefold nature of this award. Recipients excel in all three of the main waterfront activities, attaining the highest levels in each: Master Canoeist, Skipper, and Bronze Medallion. The roster is short, but it includes campers as young as thirteen.

The Arowhon A The highest swimming award at Arowhon is the A. It was devised by Tommy Walker, Olympic medalist and coach of the 1924 Olympic swim team, who was an assistant camp director before World War II. It is unique to Arowhon and some campers have worked for four years to perfect their dives and strokes for this style award. Only the camp director can pass candidates. One of Arowhon's campers last summer, Nicole, described the yellow felt A that is presented in recognition of this great achievement: "It doesn't mean anything outside, but it's so important here."

The Boulé Wapomeo initiated a camper canoe race around the islands in the late 1970s. Today, there is one course for the younger girls and a second for the seniors and staff. The winners' names and times are recorded on the roster in the dining hall. A guide suggested the name when he urged on his campers after a portage with his own phrase: "Let's boulé." He may have been thinking of the French word for cannonball–*boulet*–and blasting off from the landing.

Camp Bar Mitzvah As Senior Director David Bale says of Tamakwa, "We like to think of ourselves as a big family." When one of the family members is at camp for his or her thirteenth summer, there's a special Camp Bar Mitzvah celebration. The date is kept secret, but it's always held on a Friday, when the whole camp regularly gathers for a service on the Slope. The celebrant's real family and city friends are invited, too, and many have travelled hundreds of miles just to be there on this special occasion. Amid speeches and roasts, a spirit of genuine fondness for this member of the family pervades the celebration.

The Forestry Rolls There are three groupings of campers at Northway that have more to do with a girl's contribution to the smooth running of

A Camp Bar Mitzvah on the Slope celebrates a Tamakwan's thirteenth summer.

camp than with any specific skill. Based on Fanny Case's oft-quoted maxim, "The seeing eye and the willing hand," girls help out by being members of one of these groups. At first, a camper becomes a Wee Woodsman. They conduct inspections every morning and, when a Woodsman seems to be particularly conscientious, she is invited to become a Junior Forester. The Junior Foresters oversee other tasks, including putting out and bringing in the boats and canoes each day. The highest honour is to be asked to join the Senior Foresters. The nomination is announced at a campfire and a special poem is recited: "A good friend is hard to come by, yet she is one to many." The Senior Foresters hold the greatest responsibility around camp: they help to put the younger girls to bed, run the tuck store, and cook the final banquet. As the presentation speech summarizes, "A new Senior Forester is someone special. We give this to her with all our love."

The Pathfinder Tripping Award.

Recipients' names go back to 1944.

Pathfinder Award At the end of each summer, Pathfinder boys conduct a secret ballot and the Pathfinder Award is presented to the camper elected by his peers as the best all-round camper. The recipient exhibits outstanding personal qualities and leadership potential. His name is put on a small white plaque that is added to the distinguished collection, reaching back to 1944, that hangs on the north wall of the dining hall.

Pathfinder Tripping Award Two two-dimensional red canoes stretch across beams in the dining hall. Tacked to both are small white paddles, each labelled with a year and a name. The dates go back to 1944 and the names on those paddles represent the best trippers as selected by the staff each summer. It is a record of the boys who have excelled at what the Pathfinder clan considers the most important aspect of camp—canoe trips.

The Stilson An event rich in tradition at Ahmek is the Stilson canoe race. It was started by Tom Sanderson, Ebby Crawford, and Chuck Watson as a challenge to male staff to get in shape, and the name comes from the wrench selected as an impromptu trophy. Wapomeo guides and Ahmek staff compete in two-man teams, some of whom take training very seriously. The course combines paddling and a portage, and the final canoe sprint brings the exhausted participants under the Trading Post Bridge.

Tanamakoon Tripper Two bronze paddles inscribed with the names of the best canoe trippers in past years hang in the lodge. The Tanamakoon Tripper is "awarded to a camper who is an expert paddler and whose skill, knowledge and spirit make an outstanding contribution to any canoe trip." The first paddle was presented by Nancy Fairlea in 1950. The second paddle chronicles the most recent recipients.

Voyageurs The highest honour for a Northway camper is to be named a Voyageur. The Voyageur is not strictly earned, as is the Lone Paddler award; it is only conferred in years when a Northway camper has the best skills and also meets the criteria set out by Fanny Case:

A "Voyageur" is a Northway Camper who loves canoes. She loves to take care of them and keep them in good repair. She loves to use them and to try out all their possibilities. She tries to get a wide experience of camping through their use. She loves to help others to enjoy them.

A "Voyageur" is an expert paddler with strength, endurance, and courage to face emergencies. A "Voyageur" has good sense and uses it. She can be trusted with the care of other campers in canoes and on trips. She may paint a purple V on her paddle.

The Wilson As in most brother-sister relationships, there's a bit of healthy competition between Ahmek and Wapomeo. At the end of August, sailors from both camps compete for the Wilson Trophy. It was introduced in 1933 by Hugh Wilson, a visiting R. C. Y. C. sailor who wanted to spark keener interest in racing on Canoe Lake. The Wilson has grown over the years into an Olympic-style event of several races, and in the days leading up to it, the girls can be heard singing, "Wap will win the Wilson...." Of course, the Ahmek skippers always blame Wapomeo victories on the girls' weight advantage in lighter winds.

The Worthy Woodsman In Tanamakoon's lodge, close to the Tripper paddles, hang two bronze hatchets engraved with names that date back to 1934. "The Worthy Woodsman," the inscription reads, "is awarded to an outstanding camper who is skilled in all phases of woodcraft, is enthusiastic, knows and loves the woods and takes responsibility regarding other people." Not necessarily awarded every year, the presentation is only made at final council fire in years when a camper of the highest skill level also meets this criteria. The recipient receives a silver pin in the shape of an axe. In 1993, there were only two former Woodsman recipients at camp. One, Sarah Truscott, says, "It's such an honour....I truly respect the names on that hatchet, and I felt really privileged to receive it." Patti Thom is the other, and she elaborates, "When the senior staff in camp bestowed that award on me, it made me think somebody believed in me. I always wear this pin. You believe in what it stands for and you're proud of it. It never goes away."

"Light we now the council fire...." Tike Statten leads Indian Council Ring.

CEREMONIES AND EVENTS Special events are a big part of camp memories. Some mark the beginning or the end of the summer; others occur at more regular intervals. Many have borrowed from or modified aspects of native Canadian cultures. This "playing Indian" has drawn criticism in recent years, but many of these events were developed in an era of romanticism regarding aboriginal culture, and a hodge-podge of pseudo-native rituals was the result. It is important to view the camp ceremonies in the spirit in which they were intended—as an expression of the magic of the woods and respect for the natural world. The camps adopted a mixture of native customs as the best embodiment of that spirit.

Indian Council Ring Taylor Statten wanted to make Ahmek a woodcraft camp, and emphasis on native lore seemed to be the best way of achieving an air of mystery and reverence for nature. The Chief drew heavily on Ernest Thompson Seton's knowledge of the subject, and in 1922, the first Indian Councils were introduced with

Wap and Ahmek campers and staff compete in the water-boiling contest at Council Ring. Winners' times are recorded on a roster in the dining hall each year.

Seton's direct involvement. The original ring was beside the dining hall. The campers used to walk under a totem pole, carved by John Ridpath, to enter the area enclosed by palisades. When the council ring was moved to a more remote, forested hill after the war, the totem found its present home atop the Trading Post. In 1993, an exchange between the Golden Lake First Nation and the camps was initiated. A group of staff attended the Golden Lake Powwow in August, and there are hopes of bringing some Golden Lake children to camp in future years. The camp would like the nation's help in ensuring that Council Ring achieves its intention to honour native people, says Tike Statten.

In the early years, the councils were held each Saturday. Campers donned blankets, feathers, and paint, as they still do. The Chief led the proceedings, the order of which is preserved to this day. First he called the council to order. The lighting of the fire followed, either with dances and torches or by magical means. Brownlee Haydon's account in C. A. M. Edwards' book, *Taylor Statten*, will sound familiar to all Ahmek and Wapomeo campers:

Chief Norton sat beneath the eagle at the early Pathfinder councils.

The fire lit up and danced over the encircling faces of blanket-wrapped figures. A loon would laugh or call far out on the lake. Overhead the stars twinkled through the overhanging trees. And then the finale—perhaps after a fire-lighting or water-boiling contest, or after the Eagle Dance and other ancient games, and after the scouts' reports—"Oh Chief, O Chief, I saw a mink"—the finale came with the lone figure atop the Council Rock and the singing voice drifting off into the still night.

Near the end of the evening comes the time for Hiawatha to depart this world. He leaves the ring and his voice trails off into the distance, "Mourn ye not o'er my departure, Mourn ye not I go upon a journey...." Then, the young man who hopes to take the old chief's place appears high on a cliff above the assembly. As he begins the final test of leadership, a solitary vigil, he intones the Omaha Tribal Prayer. He sings, "Wakonda Dhe Dhu...Father a needy one stands before thee, I who sing am he."

Toncacoo The ancient Toncacoo lives at the west end of Source Lake on Bear Mountain. Since the 1920s, Toncacoo has come down from the mountain to take back the dying embers from Pathfinder's final council fire. On the mountain, he keeps the flame alive all winter, then, on the first night of each season, the whole camp gathers at the council ring. As the campers wait in silence in the dark, a canoe approaches. A bent figure in traditional native garb sits in the front, his head bowed over the coals he carries. If he believes the camp is worthy, Toncacoo takes the coals and lights the fire for another summer.

Opening Night Ceremony Tamakwans also look forward to a sign of a good summer ahead. They congregate on the Slope to ask Wakonda's blessing. The Chief, in feather headdress, appeals to the four winds: the west wind that he not blow too strong; the north that he not bring his cold; the east wind that he not come with his rain; and the south that he not bring fierce heat. Torchbearers appear silently from four directions. After all have intoned a final chant, they watch for a sign. If the fire starts by itself, they know it will be a good season.

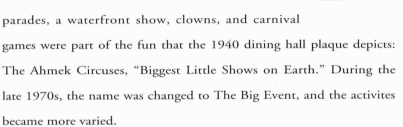

Theme Days Keeping in mind Taylor Statten's relation to showman P. T. Barnum, it is not surprising that a popular special event at Wapomeo and Ahmek was the circus. Costumes, parades, a waterfront show, clowns, and carnival games were part of the fun that the 1940 dining hall plaque depicts: The Ahmek Circuses, "Biggest Little Shows on Earth." During the late 1970s, the name was changed to The Big Event, and the activites became more varied.

Tanamakoon has several special event days each summer. Recent themes include Hallowe'en, Christmas, Commonwealth Games, and Pioneer Day. Some campers have been known to choose which month they'll attend camp based on when they think their particular favourite will be held. The girls are divided into three teams of all ages for Commonwealth Games Day. The Crees on each team write cheers and teach them to the younger girls. The events include both traditional races and wackier events. Competitive spirit runs high; it's the one time during the summer when rivalry is tolerated, perhaps even slightly encouraged.

Colour Wars Close to the end of the summer, all Tamakwa is on alert, anticipating the surprise "Break," the start of Colour Wars—three days of zany camp Olympics. The theme and opening date are closely guarded secrets. In previous years, to add to the suspense, there were even fake Breaks and tongue-in-cheek hints that Colour War had been cancelled. When the long-awaited time arrives, the campers are often roused in the middle of the night, herded by torchlight to the baseball diamond, and then treated to the Break—an elaborate introduction to the next few days' activity. In past years, the Break has featured flaming arrows, larger-than-life fantasy characters, spectacular light shows, and walls of fire. The directors claim that the past summer was the last for Colour Wars at Tamakwa; of course, they've been saying that forever.

Arowhon campers, too, are treated to fantastic breaks for their Color Wars or Council Games. Since the 1960s, they've been based on themes as well. Walt Disney, Star Wars, and superheroes have visited Arowhon Color Wars in years past.

At Arowhon the ages and sexes are mixed on four teams that compete ferociously for three days. There are guidelines to ensure that everyone participates, and the events draw on all of the skills the campers have been learning through the month. Points are awarded for each of the events and for song and cheer compositions. But, because it's worth so many points, the outcome is really determined by the final marathon. It's a relay of all of the camp activities. The grand finale happens in front of the main lodge, where four pairs of chairs stand; a string stretches between each pair, about 30 inches off the ground. Once tagged by the next-to-last teammate, the co-captains work frantically to build a fire big enough to burn through that string. In spite of an ill-timed dump in the sailing component, the Blue Team pulled through in 1993. Asked what she had learned from this high-pressure leadership experience, the co-captain gasped, "Everything," and collapsed into the embraces of her jubilant team members.

Campers and staff make gifts for Northway–Wendigo's camp birthday dinner.

Treasure Hunt Lance Kennedy has been at Pathfinder since 1960, and today he is the mastermind behind an event that has been going at least since 1946. Lance's  elaborate treasure hunts take a whole day at the end of the second half, and the clues could be hidden anywhere within the area bounded by Source Lake, Peck Lake, Highway 60, and the Little Madawaska River. The camp is divided across age groups into four teams to solve the puzzle. There are fifty questions. Each leads to the next step and is worth a certain number of points. Many involve complex calculations and incredibly cryptic clues. Even after working from 9 a.m. to 9 p.m. on solutions, paddling all over the lake, and tramping through the forest, the teams are often reduced to wild guesses at the end. It's rumoured that Lance dedicates his whole drive home to Tennessee at the end of each summer to the crafty machinations of the bonus question.

Final Banquet All of the camps have a special final meal at the end of the session, and they usually entail a lavish spread and some imaginative themes. At Tanamakoon, the counsellors work in secret up until the second-last night of camp. When the campers arrive for dinner that evening, the dining room has been magically transformed. There are floor-to-ceiling wall hangings, and favours or fanciful centrepieces on each table. After banquet, each girl receives a candle as she files out, and she lights it from a master candle. The staff line the pathway, and the campers walk between them down to the water. Each camper gingerly places the candle onto the lake and makes a wish as it gently floats away.

Camp Birthday Dinner Northway and Wendigo share in a special evening the final night of camp. Earlier in the month, there's a secret draw and everyone picks the name of a person for whom they will make a present. The last few days are busy in the workshop as miniature canoes, paddles, trinket boxes, and other gifts are thoughtfully crafted.

The Junior Foresters by tradition arrange the dining hall and make centrepieces. They move the tables into a big U so everyone from both camps can see each other, and they decorate the walls with balsam boughs. On the last night, campers dress in special colours; first-generation campers wear blue tops, second-generation don red, and third-generation wear green. The camp files into dinner under an arch of raised paddles that have been adorned with colourful bunchberries by the Wee Woodsmen. Then all sit down to a meal planned and cooked by the Senior Foresters. After dinner, there's recognition of the best and most-improved participants in all of the activities from each age group. Finally, the secret treasures are exchanged–accompanied by more than a few tears.

LIFELONG FRIENDSHIPS A number of special occasions have reunited former campers quite some time after their days at camp. Traditions and friendships are rekindled when these old campers get together.

Northway and Wendigo have held a Post Camp in recent years, when alumni come at the end of the season and bring their families. Former campers from different decades may meet for the first time here, but there's a quick connection. As Brookes Prewitt from Northway describes it, "There's this continuity, because things have never changed." But many Northway campers have kept in close touch with their contemporaries. When Ann Prewitt was asked what made Northway special, she responded without hesitation, "Friends. There are girls I was friends with when I was a camper and they have been my friends my whole life long."

Eight hundred Tamakwans turned out for their fiftieth reunion in Detroit in 1985. Many talked about the timeless qualities of camp and about the camaraderie. A highlight of the reunion was gazing on the plaques for each year; they were all carried down from Algonquin for the evening and people looked for the names of camp friends on each. A special anniversary anthology was compiled from the best of "Beaver Cuttings." In it, Marilyn Mendelson (staff 1969-81, 86-present) wrote, "It was the summer of 1969 that turned this city girl into a true Tamakwan. I learned a great deal in those short eight weeks–to cope, cry, laugh, share, enjoy and to be a part of the 'Tamakwa Family,' a family that continues to be a strong and important part of my life."

Pathfinder has had two reunions at the camp now–one at seventy-five years and the other at eighty years, in 1993. Former campers from all

An alumni trip ends at Ahmek's Trading Post, beneath the old council ring totem.

but the first decade returned to sleep under canvas. One brought his old baseball jacket, covered with camp crests and badges of achievement. His father had expressed the wish, just before he died, that his young son attend Pathfinder when the time came. He did, and the stack of achievement certificates this man brought with him to the reunion proved what a valued experience it was. After breakfast, a gang agreed to sing the Pathfinder Camp Song. The voices were a bit rusty, but then it's been nearly sixty years since some of these men were singing here.

> *I want to wake up in the morning where the*
> *pine and balsam grow,*
> *Where the loons are calling and the sun is shining*
> *And the whole world says "Hello!"*
> *I want to tramp on o'er those blazed trails,*
> *underneath my old canoe,*
> *For it's here at old Pathfinder*
> *That the days are never blue!*
> *I want to go back every summer to that*
> *camp on old Source Lake,*
> *Where the wolves are howling and the foxes barking,*
> *And the bugler bids me wake!*

> *I want to tramp on o'er those blazed trails*
> *with my tump line on my head,*
> *And when the sun drops o'er the hilltops,*
> *Turn to my balsam bed.*

As a fiftieth anniversary gift, Tanamakoon counsellors of the 1950s commissioned a bronze sculpture by Frances Gage. It is called "Celebration." The loon rising up out of the water to flap its wings has greeted people on the main path since 1974. Ten years later, there was a reunion at the camp to mark Tanamakoon's sixtieth year. One hundred and fifty women congregated for the celebration, and even the eighty-year-olds came in by canoe. They all paused at the final approach to raise their paddles above their heads in an old-style Tanamakoon salute. There are camp-organized gatherings in the city for current campers and staff, but one group of old girls meets informally for lunch on the first Monday of every month. There are campers from the very first summer in this group, and they haven't lost their camp spirit.

The Taylor Statten camps have held several large reunions, including one to mark Algonquin's centennial in 1993. A more regular venue for renewing old friendships, though, is September Camp. Carol (Benson) Devlin was there in 1993. She had spent thirteen years at Wapomeo as camper and staff, and she wanted to introduce camp to her daughter, soon to be a camper herself. September Camp is ideal for this. All of the activities are available, families stay in regular camper cabins, and there's a friendly, relaxed atmosphere. Her husband warned the family on the drive up, "Everybody be good to Mommy; it's a spiritual weekend for her." Carol led a Morning Meditation one day. She talked about the warm experience of returning to camp after an eighteen-year absence. She had found the traditional activities, and she knew that her kids would discover the same spirit that she did as a camper. "I know Council Ring and all of the other things will still continue," she said. For her children to repeat her own wonderful experience, "All they need to do is make the friends."

TILL WE MEET AGAIN: FINAL CAMPFIRES AND CANDLELIGHT

There's a bittersweet tinge to everything in the last few days of camp. Beneath the excitement of special events lies the realization that camp is almost over. Said one recent Arowhon camper, Dena, "The saddest days of the year are the last days of camp." It's particularly noticeable at the girls' camps. The last songs of each evening grow more mellow and all of the stops are pulled on the old favourites, triggering tears and infectious bouts of melancholy.

For the last night, Wapomeo campers prepare wish sticks. Each cabin composes a special message for the coming year. The Kiowas, the youngest campers, start the procession on Main Island, swinging though the other sections to pick up the older girls. They lead all of camp to the waterfront. There the wish sticks are dropped into a fire before the girls file onto the swim docks for Candlelighting.

Final council fire at Tanamakoon is held at Dawandena, at the council ring. Songs punctuate the proceedings; there are special presentations: mugs for the men on staff, first-year pins for new counsellors, three- and five-year staff pins, and mementoes for ten-year campers. The activity leaders speak about the month's programs and special moments. In years when they are conferred, the Worthy Woodsman and the Tanamakoon Tripper are presented. The girls look around the ring at the familiar carvings and poles, and lumps start to rise in each throat. One by one, the sections slowly move off into the dark, each singing a song rich in special significance for Tanamakoon.

The saddest days of the year are the last days of camp.

"So when I hear the laughter of a buddy, And when I hear the song begin to start, I know my camping days at Arowhon, Will live forever in my heart."

When the rest of camp has retired to the tents, the small group of Senior Foresters at Northway meets for a final campfire. The girls sit in silence, reflecting on the summer's challenges and achievements, each regarding the balsam bough she holds. Whenever she is ready, each girl rises, adds her bough to the fire, and quietly slips away.

Only on the last night at Ahmek do the boys sing "The Flag is Furled." Though other final ceremonies have come and gone, these words have remained a constant part of the closing night.

The Flag is furled, the boats are moored
The big bell tolls no more,
The spirits brood in solitude, along the silent shore.
When oft upon a winter's night
Our spirit northward roam,
We'll take a cup and drink it to,
Ahmek, our northern home.

Awards Night is held on the last evening at Arowhon. Each section unveils the summer's plaque, and all of the activity awards are presented; the crowd goes wild with clapping and screaming when firsts are announced. A revue of the tunes from each of the summer's shows follows.

Then the campers leave for candlelighting. As they walk out the doors of the main lodge, they are greeted by a flickering A that stretches from the steps to the shore. Four hundred small candles burn, one for each child and staff member. The campers take their places by section, each in front of a candle, as the counsellors in training sing softly in the background. This is when Joanne Kates starts to reminisce about the summer and the crying begins. At the close of her moving words, she asks each group of girls and boys to pick up their candles, carry them to the lake, and make a wish as they place them on the water. The shimmering wave of hopes and dreams drifts out over the lake.

As the buses load on the last morning, it's a touching scene. Some campers wail without reserve. Tears trickle down others' cheeks. Last-minute jokes, handshakes, and slaps on the back ease the intense emotion of the moment. Some of the older campers know that they'll have trouble sleeping the first few nights at home because of the unaccustomed quiet. They know there's an adjustment to city life and they sense that it will be difficult to describe their summer to people who don't know what camp is all about. Autographs and addresses are exchanged, and then there are discussions about returning home. A first-year camper bubbles with resolution to her friend:

"I think I'm going to be nice to my parents when I get home."

"Why's that?" asks the friend.

"They sent me to camp."

ALGONQUIN'S CENTENNIAL AND VISIONS OF HOPE Algonquin Park was one hundred years old in 1993. There were several commemorative events, and the Algonquin camps played a collective role in the celebrations. It was a fitting occasion to draw them all together for the first time.

Many alumni made donations to the Park's new Visitor Centre. The shell was constructed with public funds, but the non-profit Friends of Algonquin Park had the responsibility of raising funds for the exhibits. As individuals and in groups, people who had been introduced to the Park through summer camps contributed to the exhibits in this world-class interpretive facility.

Each of the camps completed a leg in the Centennial Relay Canoe Trip in 1993.

The Taylor Statten camps and alumni provided funds for the Beaver Pond Diorama, and it was dedicated to the memory of the Chief and Tonakela. One group of former staff raised donations in camp fashion by embarking on a Super Centennial Canoe Trip. Eighteen Wapomeo and Ahmek forty-somethings finished up their five-day trip with a performance of their trip song in the dining halls.

A co-operative undertaking of present campers was the Centennial Relay Canoe Trip. Each camp sent out a special group to complete a seven-day leg. At the end of each segment, the trippers passed along the special flag featuring all eight crests to the next participants. The final group from Tanamakoon finished with a portage up to the new Visitor Centre.

On August 15, the camps held simultaneous Centennial Campfires. The program was largely written by a Tanamakoon group, and it celebrated the shared Algonquin experience. At each camp, groups took turns tending a communal fire, reading historic pieces, singing, and making necklaces with different coloured beads to represent each of the camps. During the vigil, the campers also recorded thoughts about their summer, about Algonquin, and the Park's future in a Centennial Journal. At the ceremony's close, some of the ashes were gathered from each of the fires.

Representatives from each camp came together at the Visitor Centre two days later. There they mingled the campfire ashes and pooled journals, songbooks, brochures, and other camp treasures and artifacts for inclusion in a time capsule.

When this capsule is opened for Algonquin's bicentennial, readers will be treated to an outpouring of genuine love and hope for the Park's continued protection. These young writers say best what Algonquin Park camps mean to them. And together, their journals form a link to future generations who will also come to know the excitement of canoe trips, the mystery of Algonquin, and that the camp they love is the very best.

Centennial Song

This is our heritage Algonquin
100 years that bind us strong
A tapestry of people sharing in the beauty
Time is weaving magic over all
The ragged shoreline lies unaltered
The lakes and rivers carved through endless years
The mighty forests stand before us
Reaching to the sun cherished by the young
As young and old share timeless treasures
A camper's spirit always burns within
Of all the memories shared together
Through our joys and tears
For 100 years
This is our heritage Algonquin
100 years that bind us strong
As years go by together
In our hearts forever
Children of tomorrow
They will show
As sure as rivers flow
They'll never let you go

Tanamakoon Counsellors, 1993

Departure day at Arowhon. Heading down the path to the buses.

"You can have your four-lane highways, And your motorboats too, But I prefer the woodland trails, And the swift green canoe."

This is my first year here and I think that it is so spectacular, especially the wildlife, and I hope I can come up here every year and eventually even bring my kids to show them how nice it is.

Chris

This is my eighth year here in Algonquin Park and it is the most beautiful place that I have ever seen. Hopefully, more people like the ones in this book will be able to learn, treasure, and love this place. In a hundred years, the Park has seen change, but it is still the same. Hopefully, in the next hundred years, it will continue to remain the same.

Pete

Happiness is going to camp in Algonquin Park.

Shawna

I've been tripping in Algonquin since I was six. Right now, my whole family is on separate trips through the Park. I've loved coming to this camp, and I'm sad that this is my last summer as a camper here.... Thanks for some great summers!

Heidi

Algonquin Park is a place where everywhere you turn, there will always be a friend.

Algonquin cabin